Obedience

Life Together Resources

Building Character Together series

Authenticity: Living a Spiritually Healthy Life

Friendship: Living a Connected Life

Faith: Living a Transformed Life

Service: Living a Meaningful Life

Influence: Living a Contagious Life

Obedience: Living a Yielded Life

Doing Life Together series

Beginning Life Together

Connecting with God's Family

Growing to Be Like Christ

Developing Your SHAPE to Serve Others

Sharing Your Life Mission Every Day

Surrendering Your Life to God's Pleasure

Experiencing Christ Together series

Beginning in Christ Together

Connecting in Christ Together

Growing in Christ Together

Serving Like Christ Together

Sharing Christ Together

Surrendering to Christ Together

building
CHARACTER
together

OBEDIENCE

living a

Yielded

life

BRETT and DEE EASTMAN
TODD and DENISE WENDORFF

ZONDERVAN®

ZONDERVAN.com/
AUTHORTRACKER
follow your favorite authors

We want to hear from you. Please send your comments about this book to us in care of zreview@zondervan.com. Thank you.

Obedience
Copyright © 2007 by Brett and Deanna Eastman, Todd and Denise Wendorff

Requests for information should be addressed to:

Zondervan, *Grand Rapids, Michigan 49530*

ISBN-10: 0-310-24995-3
ISBN-13: 978-0-310-24995-5

Interior design by Melissa Elenbaas

Printed in the United States of America

07 08 09 10 11 12 13 • 10 9 8 7 6 5 4 3 2 1

Contents

ACKNOWLEDGMENTS

It's been quite a ride ever since our first series was published back in 2002. Literally thousands of churches and small groups have studied the LIFE TOGETHER series to the tune of over two million copies sold. As we said back in our first series, "By the grace of God and a clear call on the hearts of a few, our dream has become a reality." Now, our dream has entered the realm of being beyond all that we could ask or imagine.

To see thousands and thousands of people step out to gather a few friends and do a Bible study with an easy-to-use DVD curriculum has been amazing. People have grown in their faith, introduced their friends to Christ, and found deeper connection with God. Thanks to God for planting this idea in our hearts. Thanks to all of those who took a risk by stepping out to lead a group for six weeks for the very first time. This has been truly amazing.

Once again, a great team was instrumental to creating this new series in community. From the start back at Saddleback with Todd and Denise Wendorff and Brett and Dee Eastman, the writing team has grown. Special thanks to John Fischer, yes, THE John Fischer, for writing all of the introductions to these studies. Also, thanks to our LIFE TOGETHER writing team: Pam Marotta, Peggy Matthews Rose, and Teri Haymaker. Last, but not least, thanks to Allen White for keeping this project on track and getting the ball in the net.

Thank you to our church families who have loved and supported us and helped us grow over the years. There are so many pastors, staff, and members that have taught us so much. We love you all.

Finally, thank you to our beloved families who have lived with us, laughed at us, and loved us through it all. We love doing our lives together with you.

OUTLINE OF EACH SESSION

Most people want to live a healthy, balanced spiritual life, but few achieve this by themselves. And most small groups struggle to balance all of God's purposes in their meetings. Groups tend to overemphasize one of the five purposes, perhaps fellowship or discipleship. Rarely is there a healthy balance that includes evangelism, ministry, and worship. That's why we've included all of these elements in this study so you can live a healthy, balanced spiritual life over time.

A typical group session will include the following:

CONNECTING WITH GOD'S FAMILY (FELLOWSHIP). The foundation for spiritual growth is an intimate connection with God and his family. A few people who really know you and who earn your trust provide a place to experience the life Jesus invites you to live. This section of each session typically offers you two options: You can get to know your whole group by using the icebreaker question, or you can check in with one or two group members — your spiritual partner(s) — for a deeper connection and encouragement in your spiritual journey.

GROWING TO BE LIKE CHRIST (DISCIPLESHIP). Here is where you come face-to-face with Scripture. In core passages you'll explore what the Bible teaches about character through the lives of God's people in Scripture. The focus won't be on accumulating information but on how we should live in light of the Word of God. We want to help you apply the Scriptures practically, creatively, and from your heart as well as your head. At the end of the day, allowing the timeless truths from God's Word to transform our lives in Christ is our greatest aim.

FOR DEEPER STUDY. If you want to dig deeper into more Bible passages about the topic at hand, we've provided additional passages and questions. Your group may choose to do study homework ahead of each meeting in order to cover more biblical material. Or you as an individual may choose to study the For Deeper Study passages on your own. If you prefer not to do study homework, the Growing section will

9

provide you with plenty to discuss within the group. These options allow individuals or the whole group to go deeper in their study, while still accommodating those who can't do homework.

You can record your discoveries in your journal. We encourage you to read some of your insights to a friend (spiritual partner) for accountability and support. Spiritual partners may check in each week over the phone, through email, or at the beginning of the group meeting.

 DEVELOPING YOUR GIFTS TO SERVE OTHERS (MINISTRY). Jesus trained his disciples to discover and develop their gifts to serve others. God has designed you uniquely to serve him in a way no other person can. This section will help you discover and use your God-given design. It will also encourage your group to discover your unique design as a community. In this study, you'll put into practice what you've learned in the Bible study by taking a step to serve others. These simple steps will take your group on a faith journey that could change your lives forever.

 SHARING YOUR LIFE MISSION EVERY DAY (EVANGELISM). Many people skip over this aspect of the Christian life because it's scary, relationally awkward, or simply too much work for their busy schedules. But Jesus wanted all of his disciples to help outsiders connect with him, to know him personally. This doesn't mean preaching on street corners. It could mean welcoming a few newcomers into your group, hosting a short-term group in your home, or walking through this study with a friend. In this study, you'll have an opportunity to go beyond Bible study to biblical living.

 SURRENDERING YOUR LIFE FOR GOD'S PLEASURE (WORSHIP). God is most pleased by a heart that is fully his. Each group session will give you a chance to surrender your heart to God in prayer and worship. You may read a psalm together, share a page in your journal, or sing a song to close your meeting. (A LIFE TOGETHER Worship DVD/CD series, produced by Maranatha!, is available through www.lifetogether.com.) If you have never prayed aloud in a group before, no one will put pressure on you. Instead, you'll experience the support of others who are praying for you. This time will knit your hearts in community and help you surrender your hurts and dreams into the hands of the One who knows you best.

STUDY NOTES. This section provides background notes on the Bible passage(s) you examine in the Growing section. You may want to refer to these notes during your group meeting or as a reference for those doing additional study.

REFLECTIONS. Each week on the Reflections pages we provide Scriptures to read and reflect on between group meetings. We suggest you use this section to seek God at home throughout the week. This time at home should begin and end with prayer. Don't get in a hurry; take enough time to hear God's direction.

SUBGROUPS FOR DISCUSSION AND PRAYER. In some of the sessions of this series we have suggested you separate into groups of two to four for discussion or prayer. This is to assure greater participation and deeper discussion.

AN UNSCHEDULED BIRTH, NOT MY PLAN — MARY

At the ripe old age of fifty-two, I became a new father with the adoption of a newborn son. At the time I joked that the only other new dad I knew of that was my age was the actor, Michael Douglas, and he had the excuse of a young new wife.

Now even though this child has deeply enriched our lives, having him around us all the time has been a challenge as well. For starters, when people assume I am his granddad, I have to decide whether it's worth correcting them. And then there are the thirtysomething soccer moms and dads that I rub shoulders with every week at practice. It's a subtle judgment, to be sure, but one that I am acutely aware of.

Even my own son, when we discussed adopting this new baby boy, wanted to know who was going to play catch with the little guy when he got older. Well thanks a lot! Yeah, I guess you're right, I won't be able to lift a bat when I'm sixty, will I? Of course if there ever was an incentive to stay in shape, it's this one!

But then there are those who are more serious in their judgments, thinking that we are robbing the child of a normal family or taking away a younger childless couple's opportunity to parent. One dear friend has dropped out of our lives over this, and a couple of family members still give us the cold shoulder. All this makes us check to be sure we did the right thing. Were we following God? If so, how do we move forward without guilt, self-justification, or retribution? In cases like this, you have to always go back to the original call. Was it of God? Have you been obedient? If so, then let the rumors go. That's what Mary had to do time and time again, I'm sure.

CONNECTING WITH GOD'S FAMILY   20 MIN.

Most of us know that the things that etch the deepest lines in our characters are the hardest and most challenging experiences we go through. But knowing that doesn't necessarily make them any easier. We still have to go through them. This is why we need each other especially in these times, reminding each other of God's faithfulness and helping in each other's struggle to be faithful to him.

In this session we will take an in-depth look at Mary, the mother of Jesus, and the challenges she had to face in bearing the most important child in history.

1. Take some time to introduce yourselves to each other. Then discuss what role others play in your lives during your times of testing. Do they help or hinder your faith? Share a story with your group about when someone's presence and persistence in your life was a big factor in your ability to handle a difficult experience. Or share a time when you were that person to someone else.

2. With any group, whether you are just forming or have been together for a while, it's good to review and consider your shared values from time to time. You'll find a Small Group Agreement on pages 91–92 delineating those values we have found over the years to be the most useful in building and sustaining healthy, balanced groups. It's a good idea to pick one or two values to focus on, as you seek to build deeper relationships during this study. If your group is new, you also may find helpful the Frequently Asked Questions on pages 88–89.

   After assessing your group values you might want to look at the Small Group Calendar on page 93 to map out your meeting schedule and holidays so everyone can plan ahead.

3. While you are working through the rest of this session, pass around a sheet of paper or one of you pass your study guide opened to the Small Group Roster on pages 125–126. Have everyone write down their contact information, then ask someone to make copies or type up a list with everyone's information and email it to the group this week.

GROWING TO BE LIKE CHRIST   40 MIN.

Mary may seem like an unattainable character for the rest of us to emulate. We often forget that she was most likely a teenager when the angel appeared to her to announce that she was to become the mother of the Son of God. Mary's strength of character was built over time by believing and acting under God's direction. Remember, she was chosen not because she was perfect, but because God knew she had the faith to accept his will and obey. Her obedience, in the face of humiliation, certain ridicule, and unbelief, produced character.

Mary was betrothed to Joseph. They must have had plans and a handful of hopes and dreams, like all engaged couples. All of this had to be laid aside to follow God as he fulfilled what the angel said.

Read Luke 1:26–38:

> *In the sixth month, God sent the angel Gabriel to Nazareth, a town in Galilee, ²⁷to a virgin pledged to be married to a man named Joseph, a descendant of David. The virgin's name was Mary. ²⁸The angel went to her and said, "Greetings, you who are highly favored! The Lord is with you." ²⁹Mary was greatly troubled at his words and wondered what kind of greeting this might be. ³⁰But the angel said to her, "Do not be afraid, Mary, you have found favor with God. ³¹You will be with child and give birth to a son, and you are to give him the name Jesus. ³²He will be great and will be called the Son of the Most High. The Lord God will give him the throne of his father David, ³³and he will reign over the house of Jacob forever; his kingdom will never end." ³⁴"How will this be," Mary asked the angel, "since I am a virgin?" ³⁵The angel answered, "The Holy Spirit will come upon you, and the power of the Most High will overshadow you. So the holy one to be born will be called the Son of God. ³⁶Even Elizabeth your relative is going to have a child in her old age, and she who was said to be barren is in her sixth month. ³⁷For nothing is impossible with God." ³⁸"I am the Lord's servant," Mary answered. "May it be to me as you have said." Then the angel left her.*

4. Why do you suppose the angel's greeting troubled Mary (verse 29)? How would you react to a message of such favor being showered on you by God?

5. At first, this all seems like such a blessing, but in many ways it turned out creating hardship and heartaches in Mary's experience. What do you think were the hardest things Mary had to face throughout this pregnancy and birth?

6. What are some of the "blessings" and "hardships" of being a believer today?

7. As a Christ-follower, you believe things that are not necessarily shared by everyone around you. Share a time when you have been humiliated, ridiculed, or otherwise paid some kind of price for what you believed. How important were other believers to you during that time? How did they minister to you?

8. Whatever plans Mary may have had for her life were dramatically altered by the angel's announcement. When has God changed your plans and what was the result?

9. What character traits do you think were developed in Mary throughout her life of obedience to God?

FOR DEEPER STUDY

Read James 4:13–15. With the angel's announcement, Mary's and Joseph's lives and plans changed radically. It is likely that they both endured much misunderstanding, insult, and ridicule over Mary's pregnancy. After all, the angel didn't appear to everybody! There were probably only a handful of people—even among family members—who believed what happened to Mary and Joseph. Jesus would have certainly grown up amidst a good deal of controversy in the neighborhood. His beginning was not normal in their culture, angels or not.

James 1:2–4 says that suffering and insult are actually blessings and we should go as far as to rejoice that we have suffered in the name of Christ. Now James was writing to the persecuted church, so the historical application of this teaching is obvious. But what about us today? Can we endure insult and suffering in the name of Christ? How? Have you?

In Luke 2:19, the Scripture says that after the visit from the shepherds "Mary treasured up all these things and pondered them in her heart." That's a lot to carry around in your heart for thirty years. What kind of character do you think carrying that knowledge would have created in Mary?

What are some aspects of faith that you don't necessarily broadcast to everyone? What are you absolutely certain of as a Christian that some people might find laughable? Think along the lines of faith as evidence of what we don't see.

Read and discuss 1 Corinthians 1:20–25. Are you willing to be a fool for Christ? Are you willing to believe what some call a "crutch"?

DEVELOPING YOUR GIFTS TO SERVE OTHERS   10 MIN.

Mary's life was forever altered by God the day the angel Gabriel visited her. The blessing of his words brought honor to her from that day throughout all eternity. But for the remainder of her time on earth, she would live for God's purposes, not her own. There are times when God's plans for us are different from our plans and we find ourselves needing to choose who we will serve. But how can we know what God wants us to do, or if our plans don't line up with his plans? We need to talk to him and listen for his reply.

10. A crucial part of growing spiritually is communicating with God. Developing our communication with God involves prayer, reading his Word, and reflecting on what he is telling us. As the seventeenth-century English preacher John Owen wrote, "No heart can conceive that treasury of mercies which lies in this one privilege, in having liberty and ability to approach unto God at all times, according to His mind and will."

If you engage in these activities over the next six weeks, you will see growth in your ability to discern God's will for you. We have provided a Reflections section at the end of each session. For this session you will find the Reflections on pages 24–26. Each of these includes five days of Scripture for you to read and reflect upon. There is also a place for you to record your thoughts. On day six, reflect on what you have looked at in this session and during your Reflections time this week. This important habit will help you grow closer to God throughout this study.

11. As you work through the sessions of this study you will have opportunities to set goals for growth and put what you are

learning into practice. Following through on a resolution is tough when you're on your own, but we have found it makes all the difference to have a partner cheering us on. Pair up with someone in your group. (We suggest that men partner with men and women with women.) This person will be your "spiritual partner" during this study. He or she doesn't have to be your best friend but will simply encourage you to complete any goals you set for yourself during the coming weeks.

On pages 94–95 is a Personal Health Plan, a chart for keeping track of your spiritual progress. In the box that says "WHO are you connecting with spiritually?" write your partner's name. You can see that the Health Plan contains space for you to record the ups and downs of your progress each week in the column labeled "My Progress." And now with your spiritual partner you don't have to do it alone, but together with a friend.

When you check in with your partner each week, the "Partner's Progress" column on this chart will provide a place to record your partner's progress throughout this study. To help you use your Personal Health Plan, you'll find a Sample Personal Health Plan on pages 96–97. For now, don't worry about the WHAT, WHERE, WHEN, and HOW questions on your Health Plan.

SHARING YOUR LIFE MISSION EVERY DAY   10 MIN.

God chose to use the Bible to communicate his will for our lives and provide examples that show us how to live (and how not to). In Matthew 28:19–20 Jesus tells us to go and tell others about him, to make disciples, and teach them everything he has commanded us to do. One way to obey him is to share our lives with other people, including telling them the story of how Jesus has changed us.

12. We've found that groups that focus on reaching out to unbelievers grow much deeper in their relationships than those which look only inward. Who are the people in your life who need to meet Jesus or know him more deeply? The Circles of Life diagram on page 20 will help you think of the various people you come in contact with on a regular basis. Prayerfully write down two or three names in each of the circles.

CIRCLES OF LIFE

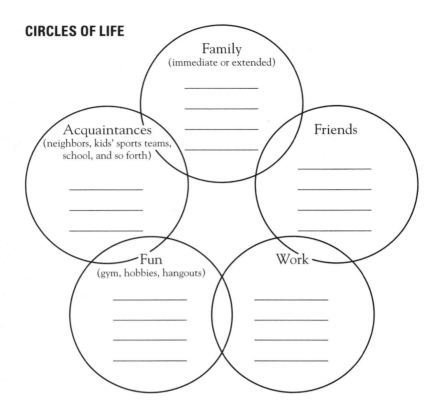

The beginning of a new study is a wonderful time to welcome a few friends into your group. Which of the people in your circles could you invite? Like the friends of the paralytic in Mark 2, help your friends overcome obstacles to attending your group. Do they need a ride to the group? Help with child care? What can you, or your group, do to help?

13. Is there someone whom you wouldn't invite to your group but who still needs a connection? Would you be willing to have lunch or coffee with that person, catch up on life, and share something you've learned from this study?

SURRENDERING YOUR LIFE FOR GOD'S PLEASURE   15–20 MIN.

It is clear that God wants us to share with others what Jesus has done in our lives. As a group, begin to pray for an awareness of those around you with whom God would like you to share your story.

14. Share your prayer requests and take a few minutes to pray together as a group. Each person pray one- or two-sentence prayers. Pray that you would be willing, open, and responsive to God's leading in your life. Ask God to show you this week how, when, and what you can share that will touch the hearts of people around you. Pray especially for the hearts of those God revealed to you during the Circles of Life exercise on page 20. Be sure to write your prayer requests on the Prayer and Praise Report on page 23.

15. Remember to use the Reflections verses at the end of this session in your quiet time this week. Record any thoughts or direction you receive from the Lord in the space provided.

STUDY NOTES

A virgin. The Greek word used here is *partheon*, which literally means a "maiden." The implication is that this is an unmarried daughter or virgin. This word is consistently translated as "virgin" throughout the New Testament and even is used to describe a chaste man in Revelation 14:4 as well as in other Greek literature of the time.

Pledged to be married. The engagement period was regarded as a promise of mutual fidelity. Any relationship outside of this marriage pledge would have been regarded as adultery (Deuteronomy 22:13ff). A formal divorce was required to end the engagement.

Was greatly troubled. The glorious appearance of God's messenger filled Mary with amazement, and she didn't know what to think about the angel's words.

Give him the name Jesus. The name "Jesus" is derived from the Hebrew name "Joshua," meaning "the Lord is salvation." The meaning might have been lost on Luke's Gentile Christian audience, but the meaning is highly significant today.

Throne of his father David. This announcement by the angel fulfills the promise to David that his kingdom would last forever (2 Samuel 7:16) as well as fulfilling the promise that the Messiah would come through the lineage of David (Ezekiel 37:24).

Holy Spirit will come upon you ... power of the Most High will overshadow you ... the holy one to be born will be called the Son of God. This is a miraculous occurrence. There is no other explanation for how a virgin could become pregnant, let alone bear the Son of God. While we do not understand the "how" of this miracle, this act of the Trinity (Holy Spirit, the Most High, and the Son of God) produced a sinless God-man who was not subjected to the taint of a son of Adam.

Briefly share your prayer requests with the large group, making notations below. Then gather in small groups of two to four to pray for each other.

Date: 9-10-12

PRAYER REQUESTS

Seth O.
Becky sugar
Church bills
John French
Monica Mom surg 27
Melie surgery 10-9
Pray at th pole breakfast next week
Rebeck having proble with baby
Embercy probles
Mel new job
Kylie eye Dr

PRAISE REPORT

REFLECTIONS

Each day read the daily verse(s) and give prayerful consideration to what you learn about God, his Spirit, and his place in your life. Then record your thoughts, insights, or prayer in the Reflect section. On day six record a summary of what you have learned over the entire week through this study.

DAY 1   *"Consider it all joy, my brethren, when you encounter various trials, knowing that the testing of your faith produces endurance. And let endurance have its perfect result, that you may be perfect and complete, lacking in nothing." (James 1:2–4 NASB)*

REFLECT: *When I had testing I know God will be with me all the way.*

DAY 2   *"Now listen, you who say, 'Today or tomorrow we will go to this or that city, spend a year there, carry on business and make money.' Why, you do not even know what will happen tomorrow. What is your life? You are a mist that appears for a little while and then vanishes." (James 4:13–14)*

REFLECT: *I have been trying to say God willing I will go somewhere or do this or that.*

DAY 3   *"I will sing to the LORD all my life; I will sing praise to my God as long as I live. May my meditation be pleasing to him, as I rejoice in the LORD. But may sinners vanish from the earth and the wicked be no more." (Psalm 104:33–35)*

REFLECT: _____

_____

_____

_____

_____

_____

_____

_____

_____

_____

_____

DAY 4   *"Great is the LORD and most worthy of praise; his greatness no one can fathom." (Psalm 145:3)*

REFLECT: _____

_____

_____

_____

_____

_____

_____

_____

_____

_____

_____

DAY 5 *" Speaking to one another in psalms and hymns and spiritual songs, singing and making melody with your heart to the Lord; always giving thanks for all things in the name of our Lord Jesus Christ to God, even the Father." (Ephesians 5:19 – 20 NASB)*

REFLECT: _____

_____

_____

_____

_____

_____

_____

_____

_____

_____

_____

DAY 6 Use the following space to write any thoughts God has put in your heart and mind about the things discussed during session one and/or during your Reflections time this week.

SUMMARY: _____

_____

_____

_____

_____

_____

_____

_____

_____

_____

YOU CAN HAVE MY SON — ABRAHAM

I have experienced the loss through death of three friends and coworkers in the kingdom of God that has left me experiencing everything from wondering why to extreme anger, and all points in-between. These were talented people with numerous gifts useful to the body of Christ and the world. They also had a perspective on the world that few have, and one I believe is much needed among followers of Christ. "If you're going to take somebody," I have asked God on numerous occasions, "why someone so crucial to your work in the world?" The temptation is to wonder about whether God has a clear idea about what he is doing. Of course this is a ridiculous assumption, but I am human and I see God in my terms, not his.

In times like these, I have to let God be God and try not to question him. I have a right to tell him how I feel — certainly he can handle that — but the issues of faith and trust need to be upheld. When I am tempted to lose faith in God, I need to affirm his sovereignty amidst my own doubt and confusion.

God has heard from me in no uncertain terms about his taking these three, but my confidence in him, and in the knowledge that he is working out his perfect will in the world, has gone unshaken. It ultimately comes down to the fact that God is God and I am not. I will trust him even though I don't get what he is doing, or like it either. I notice he didn't consult with me first about these things, and why should he?

CONNECTING WITH GOD'S FAMILY   20 MIN.

Would God ever ask us to give up our most prized possession? Would he ever ask us to give up even what we thought *he* had given us? He might. He asked this of Abraham. He might be testing our love (do we have any other gods before him?), and he might be testing our faith (do we believe him regardless?), but he doesn't do this just to play games with us. He does it to make us strong — to build up character in us that enables us to trust him no matter what. This session we will explore what happens when God asks us to surrender something dear to our hearts.

1. If new people have joined the group, be sure that whoever invited them introduces them to the rest of the group. Then a few of you answer the question: Other than a person, what is your most prized possession? *God, my Bible, my family.*

    Have you ever lost anything that was very important to you? Share with the group what you lost and how the loss affected you. Did you ever get it back? How did you feel then? *I lost my wedding ring. I looked everywhere. I found in my pants pocket. I was very glad*

2. Sit with your spiritual partner. On pages 98–99 of this study guide you'll find the Personal Health Assessment. Take a few minutes right now to rate yourself in each area. You won't have to share your scores with the group. Discuss the following with your spiritual partner:

    -   What's one area that is going well and one area that's not going as well? Don't be embarrassed; everybody struggles in one area or another.

    -   Take a moment and write in a simple step (or goal) under "WHAT is your next step for growth?" on the Personal Health Plan on page 98.

    Share your goal with your spiritual partner and plan to give updates on your progress throughout this study.

GROWING TO BE LIKE CHRIST   40 MIN.

Few tests God has ever asked of anyone can surpass the magnitude of Abraham being asked to sacrifice his son Isaac. No father or mother can encounter this gripping story without cringing over what it must have been like to go through with this. Isaac was the promised son. His descendents were to exceed the stars in the heavens. Abraham and Sarah had waited long after Sarah was of age to give birth, and God had given them Isaac as a miracle. Now this same God was asking Abraham to give Isaac back to him as a human sacrifice? What kind of madness was that? Who of us would have been willing to go up that mountain with wood, fire, and a son? What was it that made Abraham do it?

This story is an amazing test of surrender and faith. We will try to discover what elements were working in Abraham's heart to make him able to pass such a test, and how these same factors can help us in our everyday struggle to believe and surrender.

Read Genesis 22:1–14:

Some time later God tested Abraham. He said to him, "Abraham!" "Here I am," he replied. [2]Then God said, "Take your son, your only son, Isaac, whom you love, and go to the region of Moriah. Sacrifice him there as a burnt offering on one of the mountains I will tell you about." [3]Early the next morning Abraham got up and saddled his donkey. He took with him two of his servants and his son Isaac. When he had cut enough wood for the burnt offering, he set out for the place God had told him about. [4]On the third day Abraham looked up and saw the place in the distance. [5]He said to his servants, "Stay here with the donkey while I and the boy go over there. We will worship and then we will come back to you." [6]Abraham took the wood for the burnt offering and placed it on his son Isaac, and he himself carried the fire and the knife. As the two of them went on together, [7]Isaac spoke up and said to his father Abraham, "Father?" "Yes, my son?" Abraham replied. "The fire and wood are here," Isaac said, "but where is the lamb for the burnt offering?" [8]Abraham answered, "God himself will provide the lamb for the burnt offering, my son." And the two of them went on together. [9]When they reached the place God had told him about, Abraham built an altar there and arranged the wood on it. He bound his son Isaac and laid him on the altar, on top of the wood. [10]Then he reached out his hand and took the knife to slay his son. [11]But the angel of the LORD called out to him from heaven, "Abraham! Abraham!" "Here I am," he replied. [12]"Do not lay a hand on the boy," he said. "Do not do anything to him. Now I know that you fear God, because you have not withheld from me your son, your only son." [13]Abraham looked up and there

*in a thicket he saw a ram caught by its horns. He went over
and took the ram and sacrificed it as a burnt offering instead
of his son. ¹⁴So Abraham called that place The LORD Will
Provide. And to this day it is said, "On the mountain of the
LORD it will be provided."*

3. One of the disadvantages of these stories, as they appear in
   Scripture, is that they don't provide much of the emotional
   contexts. We have to read between the lines for that. For
   instance, it looks like Abraham just heard God's call and
   immediately rounded up his son and the necessary equip-
   ment and took off for the mountain. What must have been
   going through Abraham's mind as he prepared to follow
   through with God's request? Why do you think Abraham
   seemed at peace with following God's instructions to offer
   Isaac as a sacrificial lamb? *Because God had
   promise him a son,*

4. Abraham told his servants, "Stay here with the donkey while
   I and the boy go over there. We will worship and then we
   will come back to you" (verse 5). What does this tell you
   about how Abraham was expecting to come back down the
   mountain? (See Hebrews 11:19 for help.) *He knew God
   would provied,*

5. Isaac was confused by the fact that they didn't have a lamb
   for the burnt offering. In verse 8 Abraham tells his son that
   "God himself will provide the lamb." The big lesson here is
   that God knows what he is doing even if it doesn't make any
   sense to us. What doesn't make sense in your life right now?
   What does God want you to believe about that?
   *God will provied for me what
   I need.*

6. What is the significance of the angel's repeated calling of Abraham's name (verse 11)? Can you think of a time when the Lord spoke to you repeatedly about something? What did you do?

7. When we do not withhold anything from God, our faith is made complete (see James 2:21 – 22). What does this look like in the life of Christians today? *We need to have more faith.*

FOR DEEPER STUDY

Read Hebrews 11:1 – 19. Hebrews 11 is often referred to as the faith chapter, and no wonder. It begins with a definition of faith and then presents a list of Old Testament characters who are examples of what a life of faith looks like. It is kind of like God's Hall of Fame, only we'd have to call it the Hall of Faith because it is not these people but their faith that has made them so famous.

Verse 1 speaks of faith as evidence of what we hope for and can't see. Wait a minute. How can something you can't see be evidence?

Abraham's whole life was centered on God's promise that he would be the father of many nations and yet God made him and Sarah wait until well past her childbearing years to fulfill that promise. Why do you suppose God did that? Has God promised you something you are still waiting for? What do you suppose Abraham would say about that?

Would Abraham have plunged the knife into Isaac, his son of promise, had God not stopped him?

When do you suppose Abraham realized this was just a test of his faith?

Do you think God tests our faith today through the circumstances of our lives? Can you share a time when your faith was tested?

Through all of this, Abraham held on to God's promise that his offspring would be reckoned *through Isaac.* That was all the word he needed.

DEVELOPING YOUR GIFTS TO SERVE OTHERS   10 MIN.

God is more concerned about our spiritual growth than anything else, so he continually asks us to stretch ourselves to take another step toward service that may seem difficult or require some sacrifice.

8. There are many ways group members can share the numerous responsibilities involved in a successful small group. For instance, you could coordinate refreshments, plan a social event, help with prayer requests, track and recognize birthdays and anniversaries, plan a ministry project, lead part of the discussion, or respond with a meal when a crisis occurs. What responsibility are you willing to assume for the next two or three months?

9. Rotating hosts and leaders is a great place to start and one of the values we highly recommend for your group. People need opportunities to experiment with ways in which God may

have gifted them. Your group will give you all the encouragement you need before, during, and after the session. Some groups like to let the host lead the meeting each week, while others like to let one person host while another person leads.

The Small Group Calendar on page 93 is a tool for planning who will host and lead each meeting and who will provide refreshments. Take a few minutes to plan for your next four meetings. Don't pass this up! It will greatly impact your group.

SHARING YOUR LIFE MISSION EVERY DAY   10 MIN.

10. Take time now to begin planning a group social event to which you could invite some people who don't know Christ. For example, you might:

- Share a meal together prior to your group time. Ask someone to coordinate the date, time, and place. Make sure the information gets out to everyone.

- Go out to dinner together or have a potluck at someone's home.

- Plan a women's night out while the guys take care of the kids; then plan another evening for the guys to go out while the women watch the kids. If no one in your group has children, designate a night for the women to have a "girls' night out" and the men to have a "men's night out."

Or come up with a creative idea of your own. Remember, this should be all about enjoying friendship—not putting unbelievers on the spot. Let your non-Christian friends see that Christians are fun to be around.

SURRENDERING YOUR LIFE FOR GOD'S PLEASURE   15–20 MIN.

God provided Abraham a long-awaited son, then asked him to give him back, then gave him back to Abraham once more. Through it all, Abraham continued to praise God. In session one we talked about the role of prayer, Bible study, and reflection in our personal spiritual growth. In this and the remaining sessions, we will spend some time on the various aspects of prayer beginning with prayers of thanks and praise to God for his provision in our lives.

11. Break into circles of two to four people and share a few things you are thankful to God for. Write these on your Prayer and Praise Report on page 36. Spend a few minutes praising God for all the blessings mentioned in your circle. In your prayer time throughout this week, continue to praise God for what he has done in your life and the lives of the people in your circle. Be prepared to share with your group next week what, if any, effect this exercise has had on you.

12. Between group meetings, use the Reflections verses provided at the end of each session in your quiet time. Each day read the daily verse(s) and give prayerful consideration to what you learn about God, his Spirit, and his place in your life. Then record your thoughts, insights, or prayer in the space provided.

STUDY NOTES

God tested Abraham. Similar to Job, Abraham was not aware that the forthcoming events were a test by God. Similar to Job and the rest of God's people, both then and today, faith is tested in order to strengthen one's trust in God, to prepare God's child for greater works ahead, and to deepen one's relationship with God. At Sarah's urging, Abraham had expelled his first son, Ishmael, along with Ishmael's mother, Hagar (Genesis 21). Isaac was Abraham's only hope of living up to his name of "father of many nations" (17:4). At over a hundred years of age, Abraham had little chance, short of a miracle, of having another child. Isaac was the link to his promised legacy.

Region of Moriah. Mount Moriah was located near Salem, which later became Jerusalem. Abraham and Isaac traveled roughly fifty miles from Beersheba (Genesis 21:33) to Moriah.

Take your son, your only son, Isaac, whom you love. The obvious parallel here is a foreshadowing of God giving his only Son, Jesus, so that we could receive eternal life (John 3:16). The striking difference is that Jesus willingly offered himself as a sacrifice, whereas God is commanding Abraham to offer Isaac as a sacrifice. This would have been highly controversial, in that human sacrifice was a pagan rite not practiced among God's people nor required by God. Abraham's faith rested in God's ability to raise Isaac from the dead

(Hebrews 11:19). As indicated in Exodus 22:29, the firstborn son was to be offered in dedication to God but redeemed by a lamb (34:20).

Burnt offering. A burnt offering involved cutting up and offering an entire animal on the altar as a sacrifice. Abraham's sacrifice of a ram foreshadows the burnt offering of a lamb every morning and evening in the temple. There is further significance, in that the temple was built on "Mount Moriah" (2 Chronicles 3:1).

The angel of the LORD called out to him from heaven. So as not to be late in warning and redirecting Abraham, the angel of the Lord called out from heaven. The urgency of the matter did not allow time for the angel to appear before Abraham. Significantly, the last usage of God's covenant name was at the promise of Isaac's birth (Genesis 21:1).

The LORD Will Provide. The location of this event is not a coincidence, in that the name Moriah literally means "the Lord provides." Thus, Abraham comments in Genesis 22:14 that "on the mountain of the LORD it will be provided" (Yahweh-Jireh or Jehovah-Jireh).

PRAYER AND PRAISE REPORT

Briefly share your prayer requests with the large group, making notations below. Then gather in small groups of two to four to pray for each other.

Date: _____

PRAYER REQUESTS

_____

_____

_____

_____

_____

_____

_____

_____

_____

_____

_____

PRAISE REPORT

_____

_____

_____

_____

_____

_____

_____

_____

REFLECTIONS

Each day read the daily verse(s) and give prayerful consideration to what you learn about God, his Spirit, and his place in your life. Then record your thoughts, insights, or prayer in the Reflect section. On day six record a summary of what you have learned over the entire week through this study.

DAY 1 *"I know that you fear God, because you have not withheld from me your son, your only son." (Genesis 22:12)*

REFLECT: *I hope I could be like Abraham.*

_____

_____

_____

_____

_____

_____

_____

DAY 2 *"Was not our ancestor Abraham considered righteous for what he did when he offered his son Isaac on the altar? You see that his faith and his actions were working together, and his faith was made complete by what he did." (James 2:21–22)*

REFLECT: *God said he will take care of me, if I trust him.*

_____

_____

_____

_____

_____

_____

DAY 3   *"I lift up my eyes to the hills—where does my help come from? My help comes from the LORD, the Maker of heaven and earth." (Psalm 121:1–2)*

REFLECT: _____

_____

_____

_____

_____

_____

_____

_____

_____

_____

_____

_____

_____

DAY 4   *"I am your servant; give me discernment that I may understand your statutes." (Psalm 119:125)*

REFLECT: _____

_____

_____

_____

_____

_____

_____

_____

_____

_____

_____

_____

DAY 5 *"Trust in the LORD with all your heart and lean not on your own understanding." (Proverbs 3:5)*

REFLECT: _____

_____

_____

_____

_____

_____

_____

_____

_____

_____

_____

_____

_____

DAY 6 Use the following space to write any thoughts God has put in your heart and mind about the things discussed during session two and/or during your Reflections time this week.

SUMMARY: _____

_____

_____

_____

_____

_____

_____

_____

_____

_____

_____

_____

HOPE FOR THE HOPELESS — RAHAB

When I first met my wife, she was a fairly new Christian who had already created an impressive résumé of ministry. It amazed me how fast she had grown spiritually, and how much God had used her in just a few short years. She had started a chapter of an international Christian association in her field of work, she was heading up a Bible study of new believers, and already had a growing list of speaking engagements under her belt. When I found out her somewhat storied past included an unhappy list of former relationships including one failed marriage from which she split after a year, I was even more amazed. That is, until I realized how much love she had for a God who had forgiven her completely and given her a fresh start in life.

God's best servants are those who have been through the worst. Bob Dylan sang, "When you've got nothin', you've got nothin' to lose." It's this kind of awareness that fills your heart with the deepest sense of gratitude and worship. There is no deeper worship than what flows from a forgiven heart. "Lord, have mercy on me, a sinner" is the prayer that will be heard the quickest in heaven. We're all underdogs who don't deserve to win, and the ones who understand that the most are people God can tap into on a moment's notice.

CONNECTING WITH GOD'S FAMILY   20 MIN.

All of God's saints started out sinners; he is the friend of sinners. The best are sometimes the worst. Those with pristine reputations and record church attendance going back more years than can be remembered often lose sight of this. These pillars of faith are not only in danger of forgetting their past sin, but also of overlooking their current sin. A big part of character is never losing sight of the fact that one has been saved, and *from* what one is being saved. God hears the honest prayer of the sinner calling out for his mercy and is deaf to the prideful judgments of the self-proclaimed righteous. Often there's more potential for godliness in an AA meeting than there is in many churches. From the heart of a forgiven sinner comes a depth of love and mercy that only happens in one who has "been there."

Proof of this comes from something as basic as the genealogy of Jesus recorded in the opening chapter of Matthew. Out of forty-two generations, only four women are mentioned other than Mary, the mother of Jesus: Tamar, Rahab, Ruth, and Bathsheba (Solomon's mother). Three of these women were Gentiles: one was a prostitute and one was an adulteress. None of these women, according to Mosaic law, were worthy of being forebears of the Messiah, yet the Lord chose to build his royal lineage through these unlikely women. Go figure.

God's love is, first of all, redemptive, and that's the message he wanted to weave even into the human line of Christ. Joseph, the stepfather of Jesus, came from a long line of sinners, like the rest of us, and that's the way God wanted it. Jesus is the Savior of those who are drowning. How quickly we forget that salvation is the name of the game precisely because we all need it.

1. Welcome any newcomers to the group and have them introduce themselves. Then discuss the following questions:

   Why do we downplay our own importance to God when the Bible is full of stories like these?

   Are you letting God use you? How?

2. Check in with your spiritual partner, or with another partner if yours is absent. Share with your partner your progress in working on the goal you set for yourself last week. What obstacles hindered you from following through this week? Make a note about your partner's progress and how you can pray for him or her this week.

GROWING TO BE LIKE CHRIST   40 MIN.

Rahab was a prostitute from Jericho who, in return for harboring two spies from Israel, was spared, along with her family, when God delivered Jericho into the hands of Joshua and the children of

Israel: "But Joshua spared Rahab the prostitute, with her family and all who belonged to her, because she hid the men Joshua had sent as spies to Jericho—and she lives among the Israelites to this day" (Joshua 6:25).

Read Joshua 2:1–16:

> Then Joshua son of Nun secretly sent two spies from Shit-tim. "Go, look over the land," he said, "especially Jericho." So they went and entered the house of a prostitute named Rahab and stayed there. ²The king of Jericho was told, "Look! Some of the Israelites have come here tonight to spy out the land." ³So the king of Jericho sent this message to Rahab: "Bring out the men who came to you and entered your house, because they have come to spy out the whole land." ⁴But the woman had taken the two men and hidden them. She said, "Yes, the men came to me, but I did not know where they had come from. ⁵At dusk, when it was time to close the city gate, the men left. I don't know which way they went. Go after them quickly. You may catch up with them." ⁶(But she had taken them up to the roof and hidden them under the stalks of flax she had laid out on the roof.) ⁷So the men set out in pursuit of the spies on the road that leads to the fords of the Jordan, and as soon as the pursuers had gone out, the gate was shut. ⁸Before the spies lay down for the night, she went up on the roof ⁹and said to them, "I know that the LORD has given this land to you and that a great fear of you has fallen on us, so that all who live in this country are melting in fear because of you. ¹⁰We have heard how the LORD dried up the water of the Red Sea for you when you came out of Egypt, and what you did to Sihon and Og, the two kings of the Amorites east of the Jordan, whom you completely destroyed. ¹¹When we heard of it, our hearts melted and everyone's courage failed because of you, for the LORD your God is God in heaven above and on the earth below. ¹²Now then, please swear to me by the LORD that you will show kindness to my family, because I have shown kindness to you. Give me a sure sign ¹³that you will spare the lives of my father and mother, my brothers and sisters, and all who belong to them, and that you will save us

*from death." ¹⁴"Our lives for your lives!" the men assured
her. "If you don't tell what we are doing, we will treat you
kindly and faithfully when the LORD gives us the land." ¹⁵So
she let them down by a rope through the window, for the
house she lived in was part of the city wall. ¹⁶Now she had
said to them, "Go to the hills so the pursuers will not find
you. Hide yourselves there three days until they return, and
then go on your way."*

3. Verse 1 says that the spies entered the house of a prostitute.
   What do you think that means? (See the Study Notes for help.)

4. Rahab did not know the spies, but she knew their God. How
   do you think this affected her treatment of the spies (verse 4)?
   Was there any risk involved for Rahab?

5. Rahab's knowledge of God was probably limited to the stories
   she had heard about what he had done for the children of
   Israel. Based on that, she believed that "the LORD your God
   is God in heaven above and on the earth below" (verse 11).
   That's an incredible statement of faith. Did Rahab's knowledge of God affect her decisions? How? How did it affect the
   way she lived her life?

6. What does this story tell us about God? What is he looking
   for in those who call on him?

7. Rahab abandoned Canaan and its gods and put her faith in the God of Israel. Read Hebrews 11:31 and James 2:25. What did Rahab become?

8. If God would show favor to a prostitute and incorporate her into his plan for his people, what does that say about you? What have you been using as an excuse for why God can't use you?

9. What did Rahab give up in order to believe in the God of Israel? What did she gain in the end?

FOR DEEPER STUDY

Read Luke 7:36–47. You could almost call this story *A Tale of Two Sinners.*

• Who are the two sinners?

• What are the major differences between the two?

• Who got their sins forgiven and who didn't? Why?

• With whom do you identify the most in this story, and why?

Go back to Hebrews 11 and notice the company Rahab finds herself in. These are the heroes of the faith. You and I can write our own Hebrews 11. You don't have to be great, you just need to have a great faith.

DEVELOPING YOUR GIFTS TO SERVE OTHERS   10 MIN.

10. How did your prayer time go this past week? What, if any, effect did focusing on praise in your prayer time have on you this week?

11. Psalm 121:1–2 tells us that the Lord is our protection. The Lord was looking out for Israel when he used Rahab to protect the spies. When we pray, we often pray for protection, provision, and forgiveness for ourselves. This is petitionary prayer.

    Being human, we tend to want to be in charge of deciding what is best for ourselves and our loved ones and then we pray for those things. How can we know that what we pray for is what God would have for us? Praying through Scripture is one way to be sure we are praying according to God's will. Use Psalm 25:1–5 below and pray through it, personalizing it with your name or the names of those you are praying for.

    To you, O LORD, I lift up my soul; ²in you I trust, O my God. Do not let me be put to shame, nor let my enemies triumph over me. ³No one whose hope is in you will ever be put to shame, but they will be put to shame who are treacherous without excuse. ⁴Show me your ways, O LORD, teach me your paths; ⁵guide me in your truth and teach me, for you are God my Savior, and my hope is in you all day long.

12. Is anyone missing from your group this week? If anyone is absent, someone volunteer to call or email them and let them know they were missed. It's very important for people to know they are cared about.

SHARING YOUR LIFE MISSION EVERY DAY   10 MIN.

13. As a group, take a few minutes to discuss a project or min-istry you could do together to reach out to someone outside the family of God. This could meet a personal need or be a community outreach. Brainstorm ideas now and commit to having someone ask your pastor or someone else in leadership at your church about any unmet needs your group could meet. Be prepared to update your plans with the group in session five (the "WHERE are you serving?" question in the Health Plan).

14. Return to the Circles of Life diagram on page 20 and look at the names of those you chose to invite to this group. How did it go? Do you still need to follow up? Commit to extend-ing your invitations this week.

SURRENDERING YOUR LIFE FOR GOD'S PLEASURE   15–20 MIN.

15. Briefly discuss how you can make the most of praying for one another. Is there something you can do to maximize your prayer time as a group? This could mean making sure prayer isn't forgotten, starting a prayer chain, or sending emails for requests between meetings. Make praying for each other a priority and be sure to celebrate God's answers to prayer as you receive them. Make a habit of recording your prayer requests on the Prayer and Praise Report each week.

16. Pray together for any needs expressed in the group. Have any previous prayer requests been answered? If so, celebrate these answers to prayer.

17. Take a few minutes to talk about what it would take to make time with God a priority every day or even five or six days a week. Don't demand an hour or even a half hour of time; consider drawing near to God for a few minutes each day and gradually you will desire more. Use the Reflections at the end of each session for drawing near to God.

STUDY NOTES

Joshua, son of Nun. Joshua, whose name means "salvation," was the grandson of Elishama, the chief of Ephraim. A variation of the name—Hoshea—recurs in the tribe of Ephraim (2 Kings 17:1; 1 Chronicles 27:20). The Aramaic name for Joshua is "Jesus."

Two spies from Shittim. After defeating Sihon and Og, Shittim was the last encampment of the Israelites before they entered Canaan. Located east of the Jordan River, Shittim most likely sat on the plains of Moab opposite Jericho. The question arises, "Why send spies if God has already directed his people to take the Promised Land?" The first thought is that spies would give Israel a tactical advantage to overcome their enemy. But God had already promised this. The spies had a higher purpose, in that their work was to inspire faith, trust, and confidence in the people of Israel. Note their report in Joshua 2:24: "The LORD has surely given the whole land into our hands; all the people are melting in fear because of us."

The house of a prostitute named Rahab. No detail is given in this account as to how or why the spies sought refuge in the house of a prostitute. However, Josephus and other early sources also refer to Rahab as an innkeeper. The greater significance of Rahab's involvement with the spies is not only her insight into the state of the residents of Jericho (Joshua 2:10–11), but also her faith in God and his desire to save the lost (Hebrews 11:31). Why else would this enemy of Israel protect their spies at risk to her personal safety (James 2:25)? Rahab married Salmon and gave birth to a son, Boaz (Ruth 2–4). Rahab's faith and works partnered together to win her a place among the ancestors of the Messiah (Matthew 1:5–6). God used one of the least to perform the greatest good.

Dried up the water of the Red Sea. This is a reference to the Israelites' exodus from Egypt when they crossed the Red Sea or Sea of Reeds (Exodus 14:21). Described by Rahab as being one of the events that cause their hearts to melt, it is no coincidence that the Israelites enter the Promised Land by crossing the Jordan River in a similar fashion (Joshua 3).

Sihon and Og, the two kings of the Amorites. The Amorites were defeated by the Israelites after they refused to allow the Israelites to pass through their land (see Numbers 21:21–35).

The house she lived in was part of the city wall. It was customary in Jericho to build houses on or in the city walls. Some have proposed that Jericho's wall was actually composed of two walls with enough space between the two to build a dwelling. Rahab's house was situated in or on the wall, so the spies could easily escape though the city gates were closed.

Briefly share your prayer requests with the large group, making notations below. Then gather in small groups of two to four to pray for each other.

Date: _____

PRAYER REQUESTS

_____
_____
_____
_____
_____
_____
_____
_____
_____
_____
_____
_____

PRAISE REPORT

_____
_____
_____
_____
_____
_____
_____
_____

REFLECTIONS

Each day read the daily verse(s) and give prayerful consideration to what you learn about God, his Spirit, and his place in your life. Then record your thoughts, insights, or prayer in the Reflect section. On day six record a summary of what you have learned over the entire week through this study.

DAY 1   *"For the LORD your God is God in heaven above and on the earth below." (Joshua 2:11)*

REFLECT: _____

_____

_____

_____

_____

_____

_____

_____

_____

_____

DAY 2   *"By faith the prostitute Rahab, because she welcomed the spies, was not killed with those who were disobedient." (Hebrews 11:31)*

REFLECT: _____

_____

_____

_____

_____

_____

_____

_____

_____

DAY 3   *"So Boaz took Ruth and she became his wife. Then he went to her, and the LORD enabled her to conceive, and she gave birth to a son. . . . [This son] was the father of Jesse, the father of David." (Ruth 4:13, 17)*

REFLECT: _____

_____

_____

_____

_____

_____

_____

_____

_____

_____

_____

DAY 4   *"In you I trust, O my God. Do not let me be put to shame, nor let my enemies triumph over me." (Psalm 25:2)*

REFLECT: _____

_____

_____

_____

_____

_____

_____

_____

_____

_____

_____

DAY 5   *"Jesus said to the woman, 'Your faith has saved you; go in peace.'"*
             (Luke 7:50)

REFLECT: _____

_____

_____

_____

_____

_____

_____

_____

_____

_____

_____

_____

DAY 6   Use the following space to write any thoughts God has put in your
             heart and mind about the things discussed during session three and/
             or during your Reflections time this week.

SUMMARY: _____

_____

_____

_____

_____

_____

_____

_____

_____

_____

_____

_____

SESSION 4
SERVANTHOOD — JAMES AND JOHN

We've all seen these guys in airports, train stations, and downtown next to the newsstand. Their workplace usually consists of two or three elevated chairs on a platform so they can work at a comfortable level. The most upscale stations have plush leather-covered stuffed chairs and brass stands for your feet that put your shoes out where the shiner can work around them easily. Shining shoes is a servant's position that bears images of a happy-go-lucky soul, snapping his polishing cloth over shiny wingtips while cracking jokes or singing along with the radio.

A successful businessman, of course, would identify with the guy on the throne, never the one shining shoes. And yet, were Jesus here today, he would point to the shoeshine man as being the one to emulate. It's the closest thing in our society to what Jesus did when he washed the disciples' feet, and then he told them to go and do the same. He lowered himself to a servant's status, and then proceeded to meet the needs of those around him.

Servants always look up to those around them. This whole arrangement puts me down and the other person up. For the shoeshine man, the customer is the VIP. The customer is on the throne in the plush seat. My purpose as a follower of Christ is to put others on the throne instead of insisting on being there myself.

 CONNECTING WITH GOD'S FAMILY   20 MIN.

We live in a society where positioning is everything. Everyone's trying to climb the corporate ladder. It is assumed that everyone values the higher position. If you are offered a promotion and salary increase, there is no question that you will take it. Money has the last word and position trumps everything.

This is one of the things that changes when you become a follower of Christ. You get a different viewpoint—a different set of values, and with a different set of values comes another way of looking at things. This isn't to say you won't take the promotion; it means you weigh it against other things that are as important and sometimes more important.

1. Welcome any newcomers to the group and introduce yourselves. Then ask: Considering the way people live and the choices they make, culturally, what do we seem to value as a nation?

2. Look ahead and preview the Surrendering section in session six, question 10. Talk about which of the exercises presented there will be the most meaningful for your group to share together at the end of this study. Plan to go through the exercise you choose at your final group meeting.

3. Take a few minutes to connect with your spiritual partner or another group member to talk about your spiritual growth. Talk about any challenges you are currently facing in reaching the goals you have set throughout this study. Tell your spiritual partner how he or she has helped you follow through with each step.

GROWING TO BE LIKE CHRIST   40 MIN.

A person of character centers his or her life on values taught by God in his Word. Those values often clash with the values of the culture we live in and the people we rub shoulders with. It's only as we focus on God's Word that we have something by which to measure our choices.

In this story involving Christ and his disciples, one set of choices clashes with another. The disciples represent the most common element in our fallen humanity: pride. We can all identify with the disciples here, because we are all bent by the same sin nature. Jesus represents another point of view — another perspective — ruled by God's values. By asking the disciples to see their position in another way, Christ is introducing new character traits to them.

Read Mark 10:35 – 45:

> Then James and John, the sons of Zebedee, came to him. "Teacher," they said, "we want you to do for us whatever we ask." 36"What do you want me to do for you?" he asked.

37They replied, "Let one of us sit at your right and the other at your left in your glory." 38"You don't know what you are asking," Jesus said. "Can you drink the cup I drink or be baptized with the baptism I am baptized with?" 39"We can," they answered. Jesus said to them, "You will drink the cup I drink and be baptized with the baptism I am baptized with, 40but to sit at my right or left is not for me to grant. These places belong to those for whom they have been prepared." 41When the ten heard about this, they became indignant with James and John. 42Jesus called them together and said, "You know that those who are regarded as rulers of the Gentiles lord it over them, and their high officials exercise authority over them. 43Not so with you. Instead, whoever wants to become great among you must be your servant, 44and whoever wants to be first must be slave of all. 45For even the Son of Man did not come to be served, but to serve, and to give his life as a ransom for many."

4. In what ways can you identify with what James and John were asking? What does God do when we ask for the wrong things?

5. What was the cup and the baptism Jesus was referring to? Do we share in this same cup and baptism? Explain your answer. (See the Study Notes for help.)

6. Jesus doesn't explain what he means by the cup and the baptism, and the glib answer of the disciples seems to indicate they don't get it either. Why do you suppose Jesus let this go? Why didn't he explain to them right then what he meant, especially since he knew they were getting it wrong? What does this say about how God teaches us?

7. How did the other disciples react to James' and John's request? Why?

8. What do you think happens in our lives when we try to put ourselves in high position with God as James and John did?

FOR DEEPER STUDY

If you think of all the evil that has been done in the name of religion, you will find, at its root, religious leaders who did the opposite of what Jesus taught here. They lorded their power and influence over those under them. This is the way of the world brought over into religious institutions, and much damage has been done to the true message of Christ as a result. Now imagine, had all those leaders since Christ seen themselves as servants of the people they were in authority over, how different history would have been. Yet, Jesus clearly taught about servant leadership, and modeled it by the way he lived.

Read John 13:1 – 17. Jesus' washing of his disciples' feet was one of his last statements to his disciples before his death. The events that would rock the world were already set in motion, and Jesus left this scene as a lasting impression. He washed his disciples' feet — a job normally reserved for the servants of a household. It was so lowly that Peter protested, but to no avail.

Then Jesus said a truly amazing thing: "Now that I, your Lord and Teacher, have washed your feet, you also should wash one another's feet" (verse 14).

> What, then, is the meaning of Christ's statement: "No servant is greater than his master, nor is a messenger greater than the one who sent him" (verse 16)?

DEVELOPING YOUR GIFTS TO SERVE OTHERS   15 MIN.

9. Jesus outlines the values of servanthood in Mark 10:42–45. How do Christ's values clash with the worldly values we discussed at the beginning of this session? How do you exhibit servanthood in your home? In your business? In your ministry?

10. Take some time now to discuss what is next for your group. Will you be staying together for another study? What will your next study be? Turn to the Small Group Agreement on pages 91–92 now and talk about any changes you would like to make in your group as you move forward.

SHARING YOUR LIFE MISSION EVERY DAY   5 MIN.

11. Look back at the Circles of Life diagram on page 20 and write down some names of people or groups of people you feel the Lord is leading you to pray for. You can write the names outside the circles for this exercise. Then use this list in your prayer time this week.

SURRENDERING YOUR LIFE FOR GOD'S PLEASURE   15-20 MIN.

12. Share your prayer requests with the group. Then close your time together by praying for one another. Remember, God's power is available to meet your needs. Write down group members' prayer requests on the Prayer and Praise Report provided on page 59. As God answers these requests, be sure to celebrate how he is working among and through your group.

13. Developing your Christian life involves prayer, reading God's Word, and reflecting on what God is telling you through his Word. If you commit to engaging in these activities over the next few weeks, you will see growth. Continue to use the Reflections verses on pages 60–62 to keep focused on this important habit. Record your thoughts in the space provided. This will help you grow closer to God throughout this study.

STUDY NOTES

Sons of Zebedee. Zebedee, married to Salome (see Matthew 20:20; 27:56; Mark 15:40), was a fisherman who lived near Bethsaida. James and John are also referred to as the "Sons of Thunder" (Mark 3:17), probably descriptive of their dispositions. The brothers were warm and impetuous, as revealed in their ministry.

Sit at your right and the other at your left in your glory. James and John are innocently requesting the top seats in Jesus' coming government. "In your glory" during the life of Jesus bore the significance of the coming kingdom. After Jesus' resurrection, the phrase was used to denote the second coming of Christ. Jesus does not chastise the brothers for asking. Rather he challenges them. Later, Jesus informs them that the assignment of these seats is not his prerogative, but rather the Father's decision.

Can you drink the cup I drink or be baptized with the baptism I am baptized with? Here Jesus challenges James and John as to their preparedness to face the suffering and death that he must endure. The symbol of the cup is repeated in Jesus' prayer at Gethsemane (Mark 14:36). It is not insignificant that Jesus uses the phrase "drink the cup," a clear reference to the Lord's Supper and his sacrificial death that will bring salvation to all, and "baptized," which obviously refers to a believer's initial rite of identification with the Savior.

Servant ... slave of all. Jesus uses a stronger word here by introducing the Greek word *doulos* (slave) into the conversation. Another Greek word, *diakonein*, was a common reference for serving, which was acceptable in Hebrew culture. This idea of serving or being a "slave to all" would have run counter to Greco-Roman culture.

Ransom for many. In the first century, this term for ransom (the Greek word *lutron*) would have indicated the purchase money for emancipating slaves. Jesus' life would be the price to free God's people from their guilt and shame. His blood would make the new covenant a reality (Mark 14:24).

Briefly share your prayer requests with the large group, making notations below. Then gather in small groups of two to four to pray for each other.

Date: _____

PRAYER REQUESTS

_____

_____

_____

_____

_____

_____

_____

_____

_____

_____

_____

PRAISE REPORT

_____

_____

_____

_____

_____

_____

_____

_____

REFLECTIONS

Each day read the daily verse(s) and give prayerful consideration to what you learn about God, his Spirit, and his place in your life. Then record your thoughts, insights, or prayer in the Reflect section. On day six record a summary of what you have learned over the entire week through this study.

DAY 1   *"Jesus called [the disciples] together and said, 'You know that those who are regarded as rulers of the Gentiles lord it over them, and their high officials exercise authority over them. Not so with you. Instead, whoever wants to become great among you must be your servant, and whoever wants to be first must be slave of all.'" (Mark 10:42–44)*

REFLECT: _____

_____

_____

_____

_____

_____

_____

_____

_____

DAY 2   *"For even the Son of Man did not come to be served, but to serve, and to give his life as a ransom for many." (Mark 10:45)*

REFLECT: _____

_____

_____

_____

_____

_____

_____

DAY 3   *"God, whom I serve with my whole heart in preaching the gospel of his Son, is my witness how constantly I remember you in my prayers at all times; and I pray that now at last by God's will the way may be opened for me to come to you." (Romans 1:9–10)*

REFLECT: _____

_____

_____

_____

_____

_____

_____

_____

_____

_____

DAY 4   *"If anyone speaks, he should do it as one speaking the very words of God. If anyone serves, he should do it with the strength God provides, so that in all things God may be praised through Jesus Christ. To him be the glory and the power for ever and ever. Amen." (1 Peter 4:11)*

REFLECT: _____

_____

_____

_____

_____

_____

_____

_____

_____

DAY 5   *"Now that I, your Lord and Teacher, have washed your feet, you also should wash one another's feet. I have set you an example that you should do as I have done for you." (John 13:14–15)*

REFLECT: _____

_____

_____

_____

_____

_____

_____

_____

_____

_____

_____

DAY 6   Use the following space to write any thoughts God has put in your heart and mind about the things discussed during session four and/or during your Reflections time this week.

SUMMARY: _____

_____

_____

_____

_____

_____

_____

_____

_____

_____

_____

SESSION 5 CLOSE ENCOUNTER— ISAIAH

I was in my home office one day making a number of phone calls when an unfamiliar voice answered a call I was used to making almost every day. "I'm sorry," I said. "I must have dialed the wrong number." "Well, maybe not," said a voice, much to my surprise. "Are you a Christian?"

This was very weird. Who's calling whom here? "Yes," I said, gingerly awaiting the next stage in this bizarre conversation. "Good, then I have a message for you." "O–kay," I managed.

"Fret not. God's grace is sufficient. Serve the Lord with gladness."

There was a long pause. "That's it?" I finally managed to say. "That's it," the voice said.

"Well then, thank you very much."

It wasn't until a few hours later that I remembered that the day before I had prayed one of those desperate prayers: "Lord, you don't have to do this, but it sure would be nice if I could have some sort of sign from you." I was going through a tough time and my faith needed some bolstering. I had completely forgotten about this prayer until God decided to answer it the next day.

I knew God was in this because the three things the person said were the three most important things I need to remember all the time, due to my own personal struggles. And I remind myself of these three points to this day.

 CONNECTING WITH GOD'S FAMILY   20 MIN.

Everyone who is a Christian can point to at least one time when they had a close encounter with God. For many, such an experience was instrumental in their salvation. For others, it may have to do with a real time of need as a believer, and God was gracious to encourage them with a real sense of his presence through something miraculous.

1. Spend a few minutes sharing some of your own personal stories of your close encounters with God—times when you sensed his presence or when he did something that you couldn't explain if you took God out of the equation.

How did this experience affect your life? What changes did it make in your character, if any?

2. Check in with your spiritual partner. Share something God taught you during your time in his Word this week, or read a brief section from your journal. Be sure to write down your partner's progress on page 95.

GROWING TO BE LIKE CHRIST   40 MIN.

From ancient times Isaiah has been considered the greatest of the Old Testament prophets. He is most known for his prophesies concerning the coming Messiah as both suffering servant and reigning king. Familiar portions of Handel's great *Messiah* oratorio are taken directly from Isaiah. He prophesied in Jerusalem during the reigns of Uzziah, Jotham, and Hezekiah — when things were not going well for the nations of Israel and Judah due to the people's rebellion against God. Like all the prophets of the Old Testament, he had an initial encounter with God that constituted his calling. This encounter is what is described in the reading for this session.

The prophets frequently had the dubious honor of being bearers of bad news. Most of them prophesied during times when the children of Israel were disobeying God and going after the idols of their pagan neighbors. Their purpose was to call the people to repentance and warn kings of the consequences of their errant ways, should they refuse to listen. Over and over, the Lord sent his prophets to speak to what he called a stubborn and "stiff-necked" generation. Of necessity, prophets had to have a strong backbone, a character of steel, and a willingness to do whatever God asked of them whatever the personal cost. Because of this they are models for us, especially when believing is not the popular thing to do.

As you read this passage, look for the process involved in Isaiah's calling and how it would have prepared him for what was to come when he would face persecution for his unpopular message.

Read Isaiah 6:1 – 8:

In the year that King Uzziah died, I saw the Lord seated on a throne, high and exalted, and the train of his robe filled the temple. ²Above him were seraphs, each with six wings: With two wings they covered their faces, with two they covered their feet, and with two they were flying. ³And they were calling to one another:

"Holy, holy, holy is the LORD Almighty; the whole earth is full of his glory."

⁴At the sound of their voices the doorposts and thresholds shook and the temple was filled with smoke. ⁵"Woe to me!" I cried. "I am ruined! For I am a man of unclean lips, and I live among a people of unclean lips, and my eyes have seen the King, the LORD Almighty." ⁶Then one of the seraphs flew to me with a live coal in his hand, which he had taken with tongs from the altar. ⁷With it he touched my mouth and said, "See, this has touched your lips; your guilt is taken away and your sin atoned for." ⁸Then I heard the voice of the Lord saying, "Whom shall I send? And who will go for us?" And I said, "Here am I. Send me!"

3. What does Isaiah's vision tell you about God?

4. What was Isaiah's initial reaction to being in the presence of God? Would it be any different for us today? Why or why not?

5. Surely if anyone had their spiritual act together at the time, it would have been Isaiah. So why did he feel so unclean in the presence of God when he was such a mighty prophet?

6. What was the point of the live coals and what does this represent for us today?

7. What happened in between Isaiah's sense of sinfulness and his calling that changed his perspective; in other words, what enabled him to accept the call of the same God before whom he cowered only moments earlier?

8. What kind of character do you think this experience produced in Isaiah? How would this have prepared him for the challenges he would face as God's messenger to a rebellious nation?

FOR DEEPER STUDY

Isaiah 6 depicts Israel as a nation of extreme depravity, unwilling to turn from its sinful ways, and contrasts it with God's holiness.

According to Isaiah 6:1, Isaiah "saw the LORD." But because the apostle John wrote that Isaiah "saw Jesus' glory" (John 12:41), it is probable that Isaiah actually saw the preincarnate Christ, who, because of his deity, is the Lord.

Read Exodus 33:18; John 1:18; 1 Timothy 1:17; 6:16; and 1 John 4:12. Based on these verses, what did Isaiah see?

DEVELOPING YOUR GIFTS TO SERVE OTHERS   10 MIN.

9. Read Isaiah 6:5–8 again. It is evident that Isaiah's confidence to respond to God's call came from receiving the forgiveness that was so freely offered to him. As his guilt was taken away, he stepped forward to be used by God (verse 8b). We can become clean vessels for God's use by following Isaiah's example of confession in his presence. Do you have the same confidence before God that Isaiah had in these verses? If so, how has God prepared you to serve him? Is there a next step you need to take to answer God's call to service?

If you don't have the same confidence that Isaiah had to answer God's call, why not? If you feel you are unworthy to serve him, take some time this week to meditate on God's forgiveness, his deep love for you, and come to believe he desires to use you.

10. Since the next session is the final one of this study, plan a social time to celebrate the impact this study has had on each of you. This could be a potluck, a special dessert and coffee, or just a time for affirming one another's contribution to the success of the group. Set the date and make plans together.

SHARING YOUR LIFE MISSION EVERY DAY   10 MIN.

11. In session two we asked you to consider inviting unbelieving friends to a social event with your small group members; in session three we asked you to brainstorm a project or ministry that your group could do together to reach out to a non-Christian or group of non-Christians in the community. How are plans progressing for either of these outreaches? What have you found out about ministry opportunities in

your church or community? Continue with preparations to share your lives meaningfully with others.

 SURRENDERING YOUR LIFE FOR GOD'S PLEASURE   15–20 MIN.

12. Share prayer requests in your group. Then close your time together by praying for those needs, remembering God's power is available to meet them. Write down group members' prayer requests on the Prayer and Praise Report provided on page 70. As God answers these requests, be sure to celebrate how he is working among and through your group.

13. Use the Reflections verses at the end of this session in your quiet time this week. Record any thoughts or direction you receive from the Lord in the space provided.

STUDY NOTES

The year that King Uzziah died. Uzziah (also called Azariah), the tenth king of Judah, began his reign at age sixteen upon the death of his father, Amaziah, in approximately 809 BC (2 Kings 14:21). His reign was marked mostly by good — serving the one true God; strengthening Jerusalem's walls; and defeating his father's enemies, the Edomites — but ended on a sour note when he insisted on offering incense in the temple himself, something that God had specifically prohibited (see Exodus 30:7–8; Numbers 16:40; 18:7). The significance of the year of Uzziah's death, around 758 BC, was that Isaiah was appointed as the prophet of a people who had been given up to hardness of heart. As a kingdom and country, Israel was given up to the devastation and annihilation of the imperial power of the world. Not coincidentally, this was the year that Romulus was born and then Rome was founded shortly after. The national glory of Israel died out with King Uzziah, and has never revived to this day.

Seraphs. This is the only passage where seraphim are mentioned in the Bible. While there is some debate regarding the meaning of the word *seraph*, the closest Hebrew word is *saraph*, which means "to burn." Seraphs are described as having three pair of wings (one pair covering their faces, a second pair covering their feet, and a third pair for flight). Their purpose, as outlined in this passage, was to celebrate the praises of God's holiness and power and to act as messengers between heaven and earth.

Holy, holy, holy. This phrase, known as the trisagia ("three holies"), is used not only to emphasize the holiness of God, but to also signify the Trinity. This simple phrase reinforces both the character and nature of God (three in one).

Man of unclean lips. Isaiah acknowledges his sinfulness and his lack of holiness as a person. This does not eliminate Isaiah from God's service, but his admission does lead to a divine act of purification. As with all human beings, repentance leads to redemption.

Live coal . . . touched your lips. This purging rite by the seraph gives the prophet the right to speak on God's behalf. This act parallels the sacrifices needed to enter the temple.

PRAYER AND PRAISE REPORT

Briefly share your prayer requests with the large group, making notations below. Then gather in small groups of two to four to pray for each other.

Date: _____

PRAYER REQUESTS

_____

_____

_____

_____

_____

_____

_____

_____

_____

_____

_____

_____

_____

PRAISE REPORT

_____

_____

_____

_____

_____

_____

_____

_____

_____

REFLECTIONS

Each day read the daily verse(s) and give prayerful consideration to what you learn about God, his Spirit, and his place in your life. Then record your thoughts, insights, or prayer in the Reflect section. On day six record a summary of what you have learned over the entire week through this study.

DAY 1   *"O people of Zion, who live in Jerusalem, you will weep no more. How gracious he will be when you cry for help! As soon as he hears, he will answer you." (Isaiah 30:19)*

REFLECT: *You have to ask + belive to get and answer.*

_____

_____

_____

_____

_____

_____

DAY 2   *"You have made known to me the path of life; you will fill me with joy in your presence, with eternal pleasures at your right hand." (Psalm 16:11)*

REFLECT: *Thank you Lord for this proasion.*

_____

_____

_____

_____

_____

_____

DAY 3   *"Humble yourselves before the Lord, and he will lift you up."*
(James 4:10)

REFLECT: <u>Oh Lord I need you ever minuit</u>
<u>ever hour of every day. thank you.</u>
<u>Lift me up o Lord!</u>

_____

_____

_____

_____

_____

_____

_____

_____

_____

DAY 4   *"The promise is for you and your children and for all who are far*
off—for all whom the Lord our God will call." (Acts 2:39)

REFLECT: <u>The promise is wonderful news.</u>

_____

_____

_____

_____

_____

_____

_____

_____

_____

DAY 5   *"But we ought always to thank God for you, brothers loved by the Lord, because from the beginning God chose you to be saved through the sanctifying work of the Spirit and through belief in the truth. He called you to this through our gospel, that you might share in the glory of our Lord Jesus Christ." (2 Thessalonians 2:13 – 14)*

REFLECT: _____

_____

_____

_____

_____

_____

_____

_____

_____

_____

_____

DAY 6   Use the following space to write any thoughts God has put in your heart and mind about the things discussed during session five and/or during your Reflections time this week.

SUMMARY: _____

_____

_____

_____

_____

_____

_____

_____

_____

When I was but a young man (amazing how I imagine that being just yesterday), I dated a girl who married someone else before I had a chance to make up my mind about her. He clearly loved her more than I did because his mind was already made up. Little did he know, however, how much that love was going to be tested.

Before even the first year of their marriage was complete, she was involved in a tragic automobile accident that left her partially paralyzed and mentally handicapped. I saw her after many months of rehabilitation and I would not have recognized her as the same person. Even knowing it was the same person didn't help me in believing it. What I saw was someone overweight, disfigured, and barely able to speak — a far cry from the delicate, angelic being I once knew. All the things that made her beautiful to the eye had been altered, and it was all I could do to not turn away from looking at her.

But the truly amazing thing about this was the love her husband clearly lavished on her. He not only served her and took care of her, he treated her as the object of his desire. It was as if he saw the former woman when he looked into her face. He saw the person he loved, and nothing would ever change that. Nor was it hard for him to do, as I imagined it would be for me if I were in his place. I still marvel at him when I imagine how much his plans and dreams had to be altered to maintain this relationship. How different his life must be now from what he thought it would be.

John Ortberg writes in *Love Beyond Reason*: "There is such a love, a love that creates value in what is loved. There is a love that fastens itself onto ragged little creatures, for reasons that no one could ever quite figure out, and makes them precious and valued beyond calculation. This is a love beyond reason. This is the love of God."

CONNECTING WITH GOD'S FAMILY   20 MIN.

When it comes to building character, there is no higher manifestation of godly character than love, in that God himself is love. And as God's love, it is a far cry from the sugary, feeling-oriented infatuation that is so often portrayed as love in our culture. This is a love full of character that sacrifices, takes risks, and is extended with nothing expected in return. This, of course, is God's love, evidenced in its fullness when Christ died on the cross, forgiving the very sinners who put him there.

This quality of unconditional love does not come naturally. We are generally too self-centered to know how to love like this. Unconditional love comes from God, and thus it takes the power of God in a person to both experience it and share it with others. We have to ask for it, then act on it as it is given to us.

1. Tell about when you have been the beneficiary of unconditional love from another person. What did it feel like? How did you respond?

2. Take time in this final session to connect with your spiritual partner. What has God been showing you through these sessions about surrendering your life to him? Check in with each other about the progress you have made in your spiritual growth during this study. Make plans regarding whether you will continue in your mentoring relationship outside your Bible study group.

GROWING TO BE LIKE CHRIST   40 MIN.

No other Old Testament prophet was given a task quite like Hosea's. Hosea was called of God to marry an adulterous woman, lose her to prostitution, take her back again and again, and finally make provisions for her moral restoration. In this, of course, God was creating a very graphic picture of his relationship with Israel, whom he loved in spite of her repeated unfaithfulness to him.

This story is unusual in that it is an entirely selfless love commanded by God and carried out by one of his servants. Hosea and Gomer, his adulterous wife, were real people who lived out these things and experienced the full range of challenges and emotions in the process. As you read and discuss this story, think along the lines of this human element — what it must have been like to be on either side of this relationship. There is much we can learn about true love here, and much that can make us more like Christ if we are willing to fulfill his purposes in our own relationships.

Read Hosea 2:16–20; 3:1–3:

> "In that day," declares the LORD, "you will call me 'my husband'; you will no longer call me 'my master.' [17]I will remove the names of the Baals from her lips; no longer will their names be invoked. [18]In that day I will make a covenant for them with the beasts of the field and the birds of the air and the creatures that move along the ground. Bow and sword and battle I will abolish from the land, so that all may lie down in safety. [19]I will betroth you to me forever; I will betroth you in righteousness and justice, in love and compassion. [20]I will betroth you in faithfulness, and you will acknowledge the LORD."

> [3:1]The LORD said to me, "Go, show your love to your wife again, though she is loved by another and is an adulteress. Love her as the LORD loves the Israelites, though they turn to other gods and love the sacred raisin cakes." [2]So I bought her for fifteen shekels of silver and about a homer and a lethek of barley. [3]Then I told her, "You are to live with me many days; you must not be a prostitute or be intimate with any man, and I will live with you."

3. God sometimes requires us to do very difficult things. Put yourself in Hosea's shoes. What kind of human struggles would he naturally be up against in fulfilling such an assignment? What must his relationship with God have been like to enable such obedience?

4. As Gomer was unfaithful to Hosea, Israel had been unfaithful to God. Both are sins that begin with dissatisfaction. They are about feeling like the grass is greener on the other side of the street. What are the dangers in this type of thinking? How can we avoid it?

5. Hosea offered Gomer unconditional love. God offers us that same kind of love, only better. What makes it difficult for us to offer love like this to others?

6. What was it like for Gomer to receive this kind of love? What was her response? How did Israel's response to God's love mirror (or not) Gomer's response to Hosea's love?

Gomer turned her back on him. Israel turned their backs on the Lord too.

7. Hosea 2:16–20 spells out the promise of God's fulfillment of his commitment to Israel, and by implication, his promise to us. Notice that he is committed to us forever. God's love goes as far as making us fit to be his bride, even after we have gone after our sinful desires, as Gomer did. Talk about what our response must be to a God like this. Honestly, who could turn down such an offer?

FOR DEEPER STUDY

Read Isaiah 54:6–8. God said, through Isaiah, that he abandoned Israel for a brief moment, but he still called Israel his own. Our God is holy, and he cannot tolerate sin. Sin separates us from him and brings us pain and suffering. But when we confess our sin and repent, then God forgives us.

Have you ever experienced the joy of reunion with a loved one who was separated from you for a time? How did it feel to be separated from them? What was the reunion like?

Read the parable of the prodigal son (Luke 15:11–27). What did the prodigal son have to do to be accepted by his father?

What was he willing to settle for compared to what he got? Do you think that sometimes we can settle for something less than what God wants to give us? Why do we do that? Why is unconditional love so hard to receive?

If you had been the father, how would you have treated your wayward son coming home with his tail between his legs? What would you have most likely said to him?

Finish reading the story (verses 28–32). With whom do you identify the most in this story: the father, the son, or the older brother? Why?

Based on what the father said to the older brother — "You are always with me, and everything I have is yours" (15:31) — what was the older son missing in his life? On what basis should the older son have been able to celebrate over his younger brother's return? What would have to have been going on in his life in order for that to happen?

DEVELOPING YOUR GIFTS TO SERVE OTHERS 5 MIN.

8. If your group still needs to make decisions about continuing to meet after this session, have that discussion now. Review your Small Group Agreement on pages 91 – 92 to evaluate how well you met your goals and discuss any changes you want to make as you move forward. Talk about what you will study, who will lead, and where and when you will meet.

SHARING YOUR LIFE MISSION EVERY DAY 10 MIN.

At a time when Israel was unfaithful, God asked Hosea to take an unfaithful wife. Gomer's adultery is like the spiritual adultery of Israel. Just as Hosea remained faithful to his wife, God remains faithful to us. As the psalmist writes, "O LORD, hear my prayer, listen to my cry for mercy; in your faithfulness and righteousness come to my relief" (Psalm 143:1).

9. Although God is faithful, sometimes our prayers seem to go unanswered, even our prayers for unbelievers. Read the following Scriptures and list the reasons you find in these verses for why God may not be answering our prayers.

   • Isaiah 59:2

   • James 1:6 – 7

   • James 4:3

   • 1 Peter 3:7

Can you think of a time in your life when your prayers for unbelieving friends or family went unanswered for one of these reasons? Explain.

SURRENDERING YOUR LIFE FOR GOD'S PLEASURE   20–25 MIN.

We are reconciled to God through our relationship with Jesus. God's love for us is so great that he gave his only Son so that we could come to him. We owe him all our worship and devotion.

10. Choose one of the following exercises to close this study in meaningful devotion to God. Instructions can be found on pages 100–105 of the appendix. Each of these activities will take some forethought and planning to make them special.

- Communion—Focus on your gratefulness for the intimacy you have with God and one another through Christ as you share Communion together.

- Footwashing—As a demonstration of your commitment to serving one another, experience a time of footwashing together.

- Surrender at the cross—Nail to the cross things you need to yield in submission to the Lord. Give consideration to anything that you have made more important than your relationship with God. This could also be unforgiveness, bitterness, struggle with temptation, or even self-focus that keeps you from giving time to God's priorities.

11. Spend a few minutes in silent prayer asking God to show you one area of your life you need to surrender fully to him. It may be that you need to allow him to come into your life. Maybe you are vulnerable to a particular temptation and you need his power to resist. Maybe you need his wisdom to deal with a difficult relationship. If you are willing to make this commitment, share your decision with the group now or with your host after the meeting.

12. Use the Reflections verses at the end of this session in your quiet time again this week. Record any thoughts or direction you receive from the Lord in the space provided.

STUDY NOTES

I will remove the names of the Baals from her lips. Calling upon the name of a god was a familiar way of invoking that god's presence. In essence, the prophecy here indicates that God would cause "her" to forget all about the Baals. She would not even think of them.

Betroth you to me forever. In the marriage contract, betrothal was the final stage of the courtship process. The ancient practice involved the payment of the bride-price by the groom to the bride's father. The bride-price in this case is indicated in the phrase that follows: "I will betroth you in righteousness and justice, in love and compassion." The marriage will be permanent, "forever." The hope of the original relationship was for a faithful relationship between God and his people forever (Deuteronomy 4:40).

Go, show your love to your wife again though she is . . . an adulteress. Forbidden by God's law (Exodus 20:14), adultery was punishable by death (Leviticus 20:10). As a real-life illustration of God's heart toward his adulterous people, God directs Hosea to reunite with his adulteress wife and, more importantly, to love her.

Bought her for fifteen shekels of silver and about a homer and a lethek of barley. Hosea paid a bride-price to redeem his wife from captivity. Hosea's payment is a metaphor for God "buying back" his bride. The amount that Hosea paid was not excessive. Fifteen shekels of silver would be four-tenths of an ounce. The barley was the equivalent of five bushels or forty gallons (dry measure).

6:15

Briefly share your prayer requests with the large group, making notations below. Then gather in small groups of two to four to pray for each other.

Date: _____

PRAYER REQUESTS

Monica surery

East Coast Harricane, people in troble

~~the~~ Vote

PRAISE REPORT

Mels Mom doing good

Hip surger went well

REFLECTIONS

Each day read the daily verse(s) and give prayerful consideration to what you learn about God, his Spirit, and his place in your life. Then record your thoughts, insights, or prayer in the Reflect section. On day six record a summary of what you have learned over the entire week through this study.

DAY 1   *"My eyes will be on the faithful in the land, that they may dwell with me; he whose walk is blameless will minister to me." (Psalm 101:6)*

REFLECT: _____

_____

_____

_____

_____

_____

_____

_____

_____

_____

DAY 2   *"From this man's [David's] descendants God has brought to Israel the Savior Jesus, as he promised." (Acts 13:23)*

REFLECT: _____

_____

_____

_____

_____

_____

_____

_____

_____

DAY 3   *"O LORD, hear my prayer, listen to my cry for mercy; in your faith-*
fulness and righteousness come to my relief." (Psalm 143:1)

REFLECT: _____

_____

_____

_____

_____

_____

_____

_____

_____

_____

_____

_____

DAY 4   *"For no matter how many promises God has made, they are 'Yes' in*
Christ. And so through him the 'Amen' is spoken by us to the glory
of God." (2 Corinthians 1:20)

REFLECT: _____

_____

_____

_____

_____

_____

_____

_____

_____

_____

_____

DAY 5   *"No temptation has seized you except what is common to man. And God is faithful; he will not let you be tempted beyond what you can bear. But when you are tempted, he will also provide a way out so that you can stand up under it." (1 Corinthians 10:13)*

REFLECT: _____

_____

_____

_____

_____

_____

_____

_____

_____

_____

_____

_____

DAY 6   Use the following space to write any thoughts God has put in your heart and mind about the things discussed during session six and/or during your Reflections time this week.

SUMMARY: _____

_____

_____

_____

_____

_____

_____

_____

_____

_____

_____

APPENDIX

FREQUENTLY ASKED QUESTIONS

WHAT DO WE DO ON THE FIRST NIGHT OF OUR GROUP?

Like all fun things in life — have a party! A "get to know you" coffee, dinner, or dessert is a great way to launch a new study. You may want to review the Small Group Agreement (pages 91 – 92) and share the names of a few friends you can invite to join you. But most importantly, have fun before your study time begins.

WHERE DO WE FIND NEW MEMBERS FOR OUR GROUP?

This can be troubling, especially for new groups that have only a few people or for existing groups that lose a few people along the way. We encourage you to pray with your group and then brainstorm a list of people from work, church, your neighborhood, your children's school, family, the gym, and so forth. Then have each group member invite several of the people on his or her list. Another good strategy is to ask church leaders to make an announcement or allow a bulletin insert.

No matter how you find members, it's vital that you stay on the lookout for new people to join your group. All groups tend to go through healthy attrition — the result of moves, releasing new leaders, ministry opportunities, and so forth — and if the group gets too small, it could be at risk of shutting down. If you and your group stay open, you'll be amazed at the people God sends your way. The next person just might become a friend for life. You never know!

HOW LONG WILL THIS GROUP MEET?

It's totally up to the group — once you come to the end of this six-week study. Most groups meet weekly for at least their first six weeks, but every other week can work as well. We strongly recommend that the group meet for the first six months on a weekly basis if at all possible. This allows for continuity, and if people miss a meeting they aren't gone for a whole month.

At the end of this study, each group member may decide if he or she wants to continue on for another six-week study. Some groups launch relationships for years to come, and others are stepping-stones into another group experience. Either way, enjoy the journey.

CAN WE DO THIS STUDY ON OUR OWN?

Absolutely! This may sound crazy but one of the best ways to do this study is not with a full house but with a few friends. You may choose to gather with one other couple who would enjoy going to the movies or having a quiet dinner and then walking through this study. Jesus will be with you even if there are only two of you (Matthew 18:20).

WHAT IF THIS GROUP IS NOT WORKING FOR US?

You're not alone! This could be the result of a personality conflict, life stage difference, geographical distance, level of spiritual maturity, or any number of things. Relax. Pray for God's direction, and at the end of this six-week study, decide whether to continue with this group or find another. You don't buy the first car you look at or marry the first person you date, and the same goes with a group. Don't bail out before the six weeks are up — God might have something to teach you. Also, don't run from conflict or prejudge people before you have given them a chance. God is still working in you too!

WHO IS THE LEADER?

Most groups have an official leader. But ideally, the group will mature and members will rotate the leadership of meetings. We have discovered that healthy groups rotate hosts/leaders and homes on a regular basis. This model ensures that all members grow, give their unique contribution, and develop their gifts. This study guide and the Holy Spirit can keep things on track even when you rotate leaders. Christ has promised to be in your midst as you gather. Ultimately, God is your leader each step of the way.

HOW DO WE HANDLE THE CHILD-CARE NEEDS IN OUR GROUP?

Very carefully. Seriously, this can be a sensitive issue. We suggest that you empower the group to openly brainstorm solutions. You may try one option that works for a while and then adjust over time. Our favorite approach is for adults to meet in the living room or dining room, and to share the cost of a babysitter (or two) who can be with the kids in a different part of the house. In this way, parents don't have to be away from their children all evening when their children are too young to be left at home. A second option is to use one home for the kids and a second home (close by or a phone call away) for the adults. A third idea is to rotate the responsibility of providing a lesson or care for the children either in the same home or in another home nearby. This can be an incredible blessing for kids. Finally, the most common idea is to decide that you need to have a night to invest in your spiritual lives individually or as a couple, and to make your own arrangements for child care. No matter what decision the group makes, the best approach is to dialogue openly about both the problem and the solution.

SMALL GROUP AGREEMENT

OUR PURPOSE

To transform our spiritual lives by cultivating our spiritual health in a healthy small group community. In addition, we: _____

_____

_____

_____

OUR VALUES

Group Attendance	To give priority to the group meeting. We will call or email if we will be late or absent. (Completing the Small Group Calendar on page 93 will minimize this issue.)
Safe Environment	To help create a safe place where people can be heard and feel loved. (Please, no quick answers, snap judgments, or simple fixes.)
Respect Differences	To be gentle and gracious to people with different spiritual maturity, personal opinions, temperaments, or imperfections. We are all works in progress.
Confidentiality	To keep anything that is shared strictly confidential and within the group, and to avoid sharing improper information about those outside the group.
Encouragement for Growth	To be not just takers but givers of life. We want to spiritually multiply our life by serving others with our God-given gifts.

Welcome for Newcomers	To keep an open chair and share Jesus' dream of finding a shepherd for every sheep.
Shared Ownership	To remember that every member is a minister and to ensure that each attender will share a small team role or responsibility over time.
Rotating Hosts/Leaders and Homes	To encourage different people to host the group in their homes, and to rotate the responsibility of facilitating each meeting. (See the Small Group Calendar on page 93.)

OUR EXPECTATIONS

- Refreshments/mealtimes _____
- Child care _____
- When we will meet (day of week) _____
- Where we will meet (place) _____
- We will begin at (time) _____ and end at _____
- We will do our best to have some or all of us attend a worship service together. Our primary worship service time will be _____
- Date of this agreement _____
- Date we will review this agreement again _____
- Who (other than the leader) will review this agreement at the end of this study _____

SMALL GROUP CALENDAR

Planning and calendaring can help ensure the greatest participation at every meeting. At the end of each meeting, review this calendar. Be sure to include a regular rotation of host homes and leaders, and don't forget birthdays, socials, church events, holidays, and mission/ministry projects.

Date	Lesson	Host Home	Dessert/Meal	Leader
Monday, January 15	1	Steve/Laura's	Joe	Bill
9-18 Monday	1	Cle.		Fred

PERSONAL HEALTH PLAN

This worksheet could become your single most important feature in this study. On it you can record your personal priorities before the Father. It will help you live a healthy spiritual life, balancing all five of God's purposes.

PURPOSE	PLAN
CONNECT	WHO are you connecting with spiritually?
GROW	WHAT is your next step for growth?
DEVELOP	WHERE are you serving?
SHARE	WHEN are you shepherding another in Christ?
SURRENDER	HOW are you surrendering your heart?

DATE	MY PROGRESS	PARTNER'S PROGRESS

SAMPLE
PERSONAL HEALTH PLAN

This worksheet could become your single most important feature in this study. On it you can record your personal priorities before the Father. It will help you live a healthy spiritual life, balancing all five of God's purposes.

PURPOSE	PLAN
CONNECT	WHO are you connecting with spiritually? *Bill and I will meet weekly by email or phone*
GROW	WHAT is your next step for growth? *Regular devotions or journaling my prayers 2x/week*
DEVELOP	WHERE are you serving? *Serving in Children's Ministry Go through GIFTS Class*
SHARE	WHEN are you shepherding another in Christ? *Shepherding Bill at lunch or hosting a starter group in the fall*
SURRENDER	HOW are you surrendering your heart? *Help with our teenager New job situation*

DATE	MY PROGRESS	PARTNER'S PROGRESS
3/5	Talked during our group	Figured out our goals together
3/12	Missed our time together	Missed our time together
3/26	Met for coffee and review of my goals	Met for coffee
4/10	Emailed prayer requests	Bill sent me his prayer requests
3/5	Great start on personal journaling	Read Mark 1 – 6 in one sitting!
3/12	Traveled and not doing well this week	Journaled about Christ as Healer
3/26	Back on track	Busy and distracted; asked for prayer
3/1	Need to call Children's Pastor	
3/26	Group did a serving project together	Agreed to lead group worship
3/30	Regularly rotating leadership	Led group worship — great job!
3/5	Called Jim to see if he's open to joining our group	Wanted to invite somebody, but didn't
3/12	Preparing to start a group in fall	
3/30	Group prayed for me	Told friend something he's learning about Christ
3/5	Overwhelmed but encouraged	Scared to lead worship
3/15	Felt heard and more settled	Issue with wife
3/30	Read book on teens	Glad he took on his fear

PERSONAL HEALTH ASSESSMENT

		JUST BEGINNING	GETTING GOING	WELL DEVELOPED

CONNECTING WITH GOD AND OTHERS

I am deepening my understanding of and friendship
with God in community with others. — 1 2 3 4 5

I am growing in my ability both to share and to
show my love to others. — 1 2 3 4 5

I am willing to share my real needs for prayer and
support from others. — 1 2 3 4 5

I am resolving conflict constructively and am
willing to forgive others. — 1 2 3 4 5

CONNECTING TOTAL _____

GROWING IN YOUR SPIRITUAL JOURNEY

I have a growing relationship with God through regular
time in the Bible and in prayer (spiritual habits). — *I dont pray like I should* 1 2 3 (4) 5

I am experiencing more of the characteristics of
Jesus Christ (love, patience, gentleness, courage,
self-control, and so forth) in my life. — *I keep trying* 1 2 (3) 4 5

I am avoiding addictive behaviors (food, television,
busyness, and the like) to meet my needs. — 1 2 (3) 4 5

I am spending time with a Christian friend (spiritual partner)
who celebrates and challenges my spiritual growth. — 1 2 (3) 4 5

GROWING TOTAL _13_

SERVING WITH YOUR GOD-GIVEN DESIGN

I have discovered and am further developing my
unique God-given design. — 1 2 3 4 5

I am regularly praying for God to show me
opportunities to serve him and others. — 1 2 3 4 5

I am serving in a regular (once a month or more)
ministry in the church or community. — 1 2 3 4 5

I am a team player in my small group by sharing
some group role or responsibility. — 1 2 3 4 5

SERVING TOTAL _____

SHARING GOD'S LOVE IN EVERYDAY LIFE

I am cultivating relationships with non-Christians and praying
for God to give me natural opportunities to share his love.   1   2   3   4   5

I am praying and learning about where God can use me
and my group cross-culturally for missions.   1   2   3   4   5

I am investing my time in another person or group who
needs to know Christ.   1   2   3   4   5

I am regularly inviting unchurched or unconnected
friends to my church or small group.   1   2   3   4   5

SHARING TOTAL _____

SURRENDERING YOUR LIFE TO GOD

I am experiencing more of the presence and
power of God in my everyday life.   1   2   3   4   5

I am faithfully attending services and my
small group to worship God.   1   2   3   4   5

I am seeking to please God by surrendering every
area of my life (health, decisions, finances,
relationships, future, and the like) to him.   1   2   3   4   5

I am accepting the things I cannot change and
becoming increasingly grateful for the life I've been given.   1   2   3   4   5

SURRENDERING TOTAL _____

	Connecting	Growing	Developing	Sharing	Surrendering	
20						Well Developed
16						Very Good
12						Getting Good
8						Fair
4						Just Beginning

◯ Beginning Assessment Total _____   ☐ Ending Assessment Total _____

SERVING COMMUNION

The Lord Jesus, on the night he was betrayed, took bread, and when he had given thanks, he broke it and said, "This is my body, which is for you; do this in remembrance of me." In the same way, after supper he took the cup, saying, "This cup is the new covenant in my blood; do this, whenever you drink, in remembrance of me." For whenever you eat this bread and drink this cup, you proclaim the Lord's death until he comes. (1 Corinthians 11:23–26)

SEVERAL PRACTICAL TIPS IN SERVING COMMUNION

1. Be sensitive to timing in your meeting.
2. Break up pieces of cracker or soft bread on a small plate or tray. *Don't* use large servings of bread or grape juice. We ask that you only use grape juice, not wine, so you will not cause a group member to struggle.
3. Prepare all of the elements beforehand and bring these into the room when you are ready.

STEPS IN SERVING COMMUNION

1. Open by sharing about God's love, forgiveness, grace, mercy, commitment, tenderheartedness, or faithfulness, out of your own personal journey (connect with the stories of those in the room).
2. Read the passage: "The Lord Jesus, on the night he was betrayed, took bread, and when he had given thanks, he broke it and said, 'This is my body, which is for you; do this in remembrance of me.'"
3. Pray and pass the bread around the circle (could be time for quiet reflection, singing a simple praise song, or listening to a worship CD).
4. When everyone has been served, remind them that this represents Jesus' broken body on their behalf. Simply state, "Jesus said, 'Do this in remembrance of me.' Let us eat together," and eat the bread as a group.

5. Then read the rest of the passage: "In the same way, after supper he took the cup, saying, 'This cup is the new covenant in my blood; do this, whenever you drink it, in remembrance of me.'"
6. Pray and serve the cups, either by passing a small tray, serving them individually, or having members pick up a cup from the table.
7. When everyone has been served, remind them the juice represents Christ's blood shed for them, then simply state, "Take and drink in remembrance of him. Let us drink together."
8. Finish by singing a simple song, listening to a praise song, or having a time of prayer in thanks to God.

Communion passages: Matthew 26:26–29; Mark 14:22–25; Luke 22:14–20; 1 Corinthians 10:16–21; 11:17–34

PERFORMING A FOOTWASHING

In John 13:1–17 Jesus makes it quite clear to his disciples that his position as the Father's Son includes being a servant, not just the divine privileges of power and glory. To properly understand the scene and Jesus' intention, we must realize that footwashing was the duty of slaves and indeed of non-Jewish rather than Jewish slaves. Yet Jesus placed himself in the position of a servant. He displayed to the disciples self-sacrifice and love ("that you also should do what I have done to you"—John 13:15). In view of his majesty, only the symbolic position of a slave was adequate to open their eyes and keep them from lofty illusions.

The point of footwashing, then, is to correct the attitude that Jesus discerned in the disciples. It constitutes the permanent basis for mutual service, service in your group and for the community around you, which is laid on all Christians.

WHEN TO IMPLEMENT

Under "How to Prepare" for a footwashing, we'll talk about the importance of earning the right to do a footwashing. When to implement a footwashing in your "group time" can be as important as "earning the right." There are three primary places we would recommend you insert a footwashing: (1) during a break in the Surrendering section of your group; (2) during a break in the Growing section of your group; or (3) at the closing of your group. A special time of prayer for each person as their feet are washed can be added to the footwashing time.

HOW TO PREPARE

What you need:

- Towels: For the washing and drying of each set of feet.
- Bowls: Make sure you have enough bowls to be able to have fresh water for washing and rinsing.
- Liquid soap: Not a necessity, but a nice touch.

Things to be considerate of:

- The opposite sex: Men wash men's feet, women wash women's feet.
- Religious upbringing: Be sensitive to where your group is coming from.
- Know your group: Be sensitive to the bonding of your group.
- Earn the right: Make sure you have enough meetings under your belt for your group to know your heart and get the full impact of the footwashing.
- Know your options: If someone in your group has limitations (i.e., a lady may come wearing stockings, a person may have an open wound or cast) or is uncomfortable with the washing of feet, see if you can wash the hands, see if the spouse (if there is one) can wash the feet, and give the person the right to "pass."

Attitude and objectives:

- Be in an attitude of prayer for what God can do in and through you. Communicate servanthood.
- Understand the attitude of humility (both on the "giving" and "receiving" end).
- Pray for the best time to do a footwashing in your group. Timing is everything.

Some neat ideas:

- After the footwashing, you may want to give each member of your group a new pair of socks to put on to enjoy the rest of the group time.
- Before sending a member of the group on a mission trip or to multiply a new group, do a footwashing to serve them before they go out to serve.

SURRENDER AT THE CROSS

APPENDIX

Surrendering everything to God is one of the most challenging aspects of following Jesus. It involves a relationship, one which is built on trust and faith. Each of us is in a different place on our spiritual journey. Some of us have known the Lord for many years, some are new in our faith, and some may still be checking God out. Regardless, we all have things that we still want control over — things we don't want to give to God because we don't know what he will do with them. These things are truly more important to us than God is — they have become our god.

We need to understand that God wants us to be completely devoted to him. Luke 10:27 says, "Love the Lord your God with all your heart and with all your soul and with all your strength and with all your mind." If we truly love God with all our heart, soul, strength, and mind, we will be willing to give him everything.

STEPS IN SURRENDERING AT THE CROSS:

1. You will need some small pieces of paper and pens or pencils for people to write down the things they want to sacrifice/surrender to God.
2. If you have a wooden cross, hammers, and nails, you can have the members literally nail their sacrifices to the cross. If you don't have a wooden cross — get creative and think of another way to symbolically relinquish the sacrifices to God. Perhaps make a Styrofoam or cardboard cross and use pushpins to nail the sacrifices to the cross. Or use a fireplace, fire pit, or barbecue to burn the sacrifices in the fire as an offering to the Lord. The point is giving to the Lord whatever hinders your relationship with him.
3. Create an atmosphere conducive to quiet reflection and prayer. Consider playing soft music that draws you quietly to God with hearts focused on hearing from him. Whatever this quiet atmosphere looks like for your group, do the best you can to create a peaceful time to meet with God.

4. Once you are settled, prayerfully think about the points below. Let the words and thoughts draw you into a heart-to-heart connection with your Lord Jesus Christ.

> *Worship him.* Ask God to change your viewpoint so you can worship him through a surrendered spirit.
>
> *Humble yourself.* Surrender doesn't happen without humility. James 4:6–7 says, "'God opposes the proud but gives grace to the humble.' Submit yourselves, then, to God."
>
> *Surrender your mind, will, and emotions.* This is often the toughest part of surrendering. Romans 6:13 says, "Do not offer the parts of your body to sin, as instruments of wickedness, but rather offer yourselves to God, as those who have been brought from death to life; and offer the parts of your body to him as instruments of righteousness." What do you sense God urging you to give to him so you can have the kind of intimacy he desires with you? Our hearts yearn for this kind of connection with him; let go of the things that stand between you.
>
> *Write out your prayer* of sacrifice and surrender to the Lord. Your sacrifice may be an attitude, a fear, a person, a job, a possession—anything that God reveals is a hindrance to your relationship with him.

5. Nail your sacrifice to the cross, or burn it as a sacrifice in the fire. This is your way of symbolically giving to God whatever has its hold on you.
6. Close by singing, praying together, or taking Communion. Make this time as short or as long as seems appropriate for your group.

Surrendering to God is life-changing and liberating. God desires that we be overcomers! First John 4:4 says, "You, dear children, are from God and have overcome ... because the one who is in you is greater than the one who is in the world."

LEADING
FOR THE FIRST TIME

APPENDIX

- **Sweaty palms are a healthy sign.** The Bible says God is gracious to the humble. Remember who is in control; the time to worry is when you're not worried. Those who are soft in heart (and sweaty palmed) are those whom God is sure to speak through.

- **Seek support.** Ask your leader, coleader, or close friend to pray for you and prepare with you before the session. Walking through the study will help you anticipate potentially difficult questions and discussion topics.

- **Bring your uniqueness to the study.** Lean into who you are and how God wants you to uniquely lead the study.

- **Prepare. Prepare. Prepare.** Read the Introduction and Leader's Notes for the session you are leading. Consider writing in a journal or fasting for a day to prepare yourself for what God wants to do.

- **Don't wait until the last minute to prepare.**

- **Ask for feedback so you can grow.** Perhaps in an email or on cards handed out at the study, have everyone write down three things you did well and one thing you could improve on. Don't get defensive, but show an openness to learn and grow.

- **Prayerfully consider launching a new group.** This doesn't need to happen overnight, but God's heart is for this to happen over time. Not all Christians are called to be leaders or teachers, but we are all called to be "shepherds" of a few someday.

- **Share with your group what God is doing in your heart.** God is searching for those whose hearts are fully his. Share your trials and victories. We promise that people will relate.

INTRODUCTION

Congratulations! You have responded to the call to help shepherd Jesus' flock. There are few other tasks in the family of God that surpass the contribution you will be making. As you prepare to lead this small group, there are a few thoughts to keep in mind:

Review the "Read Me First" on pages 9–11 so you'll understand the purpose of each section in the study. If this is your first time leading a small group, turn to Leading for the First Time section on page 106 of the appendix for suggestions.

Remember that you are not alone. God knows everything about you, and he knew that you would be leading this group. God promises, "Never will I leave you; never will I forsake you" (Hebrews 13:5b).

Your role as leader. Create a safe warm environment for your group. As a leader, your most important job is to create an atmosphere where people are willing to talk honestly about what the topics discussed in this study have to do with them. Be available before people arrive so you can greet them at the door. People are naturally nervous at a new group, so a hug or handshake can help put them at ease.

Prepare for each meeting ahead of time. Review the Leader's Notes and write down your responses to each study question. Pay special attention to exercises that ask group members to do something other than engage in discussion. These exercises will help your group live what the Bible teaches, not just talk about it. Be sure you understand how an exercise works, and bring any necessary supplies (such a paper or pens) to your meeting.

Pray for your group members by name. Before you begin each session, go around the room in your mind and pray for each member by name. You may want to review the prayer list at least once a week. Ask God to use your time together to touch the heart of every person uniquely. Expect God to lead you to those he wants you to encourage or challenge in a special way.

Discuss expectations. Ask everyone to tell what he or she hopes to get out of this study. You might want to review the Small Group Agreement (see pages 91–92) and talk about each person's expectations and priorities. You could discuss whether you want to do the For Deeper Study for homework before each meeting. Review the Small Group Calendar on page 93 and talk about who else is willing to open their home to host or facilitate a meeting.

Don't try to go it alone. Pray for God to help you, and enlist help from the members of your group. You will find your experience to be richer and more rewarding if you enable group members to help—and you'll be able to help group members discover their individual gifts for serving or even leading the group.

Plan a kick-off meeting. We recommend that you plan a kick-off meeting where you will pray, hand out study guides, spend some time getting to know each other, and discuss each person's expectations for the group. A meeting like this is a great way to start a group or step up people's commitments.

A simple meal, potluck, or even good desserts make a kick-off meeting more fun. After dessert, have everyone respond to an icebreaker question, such as, "How did you hear of our church, and what's one thing you love about it?" Or, "Tell us three things about your life growing up that most people here don't know."

If you aren't able to hold a "get to know you" meeting before you launch into session one, consider starting the first meeting half an hour early to give people time to socialize without shortchanging your time in the study. For example, you can have social time from 7:00 to 7:30, and by 7:40 you'll gather the group with a prayer. Even if only a few people are seated in the living room by 7:40, ask them to join you in praying for those who are coming and for God to be present among you as you meet. Others will notice you praying and will come and sit down. You may want to softly play music from a LIFE TOGETHER Worship CD or other worship CD as people arrive and then turn up the volume when you are ready to begin. This first night will set the tone for the whole six weeks.

You may ask a few people to come early to help set up, pray, and introduce newcomers to others. Even if everyone is new, they don't know that yet and may be shy when they arrive. You might give people roles like setting up name tags or handing out drinks. This could be a great way to spot a coleader.

Subgrouping. If your group has more than seven people, break into discussion groups of two to four people for the Growing and Surrendering sections each week. People will connect more with the study and each other when they have more opportunity to participate. Smaller discussion circles encourage quieter people to talk more and tend to minimize the effects of more vocal or dominant members. Also, people who are unaccustomed to praying aloud will feel more comfortable praying within a smaller group of people. Consider sharing prayer requests in the larger group and then break into smaller groups to pray for each other. People are more willing to pray in small circles if they know that the whole group will hear all the prayer requests.

Memorizing Scripture. Although we have not provided specific verses for the group to memorize, this is something you can encourage the group to do each week. One benefit of memorizing God's Word is noted by the psalmist in Psalm 119:11: "I have hidden your word in my heart that I might not sin against you."

Anyone who has memorized Scripture can confirm the amazing spiritual benefits that result from this practice. Don't miss out on the opportunity to encourage your group to grow in the knowledge of God's Word through Scripture memorization.

Reflections. We've provided opportunity for a personal time with God using the Reflections at the end of each session. Don't press seekers to do this, but just remind the group that every believer should have a plan for personal time with God.

Invite new people. Finally, cast the vision, as Jesus did, to be inclusive not exclusive. Ask everyone to prayerfully think of people who would enjoy or benefit from a group like this. The beginning of a new study is a great time to welcome a few people into your circle. Have each person share a name or two and either make phone calls the coming week or handwrite invitations or postcards that very night. This will make it fun and also make it happen. Don't worry about ending up with too many people — you can always have one discussion circle in the living room and another in the dining room.

SESSION 1: AN UNSCHEDULED BIRTH, NOT MY PLAN — MARY

As a leader, your most important job is to create an atmosphere where people are willing to talk honestly about what the topics discussed in this study have to do with them. Some of you may have seekers in your group. They don't even know if they want to believe in Jesus, let alone be in your group. Be sensitive to these folks. Talk to them about something other than church, and avoid putting them on the spot with things like prayer.

Especially if your group is new, be available before people arrive so you can greet them at the door. People are naturally nervous at a new group, so a hug or handshake can help put them at ease.

CONNECTING. Question 1. We've designed this study for both new and established groups. New groups need to invest more time in building relationships with each other, while established groups often want to dig deeper into Bible study and application. After opening your meeting in prayer, pose this icebreaker question to get people relaxed and focused on the session topic. You should be the first to answer this question while others are thinking about how to respond. Be sure to give everyone a chance to answer, because it's a chance for the group to get to know each other. It's not necessary to go around the circle in order. Just ask for volunteers to respond.

Introduction to the Series. Take a moment after question 1 to orient the group to one principle that undergirds this series: A healthy small group balances the purposes of the church. Most small groups emphasize Bible study, fellowship, and prayer. But God has called us to reach out to others as well. He wants us to *do* what Jesus teaches, not just *learn* about it. You may spend less time in this series studying the Bible than some group members are used to. That's because you'll spend more time *doing* things the Bible says believers should do.

However, those who like more Bible study will find plenty of it in this series. For Deeper Study provides additional passages you can study on each session topic. If your group likes to do deeper Bible study, consider having members answer next week's Growing section questions ahead of time as homework. They can even study next week's For Deeper Study passages for homework too. Then, during the Growing portion of your meeting, you can share the high points of what you've learned.

Question 2. A Small Group Agreement helps you clarify your group's priorities and cast new vision for what the group can be. Members can imagine what your group could be like if they lived these values. So turn to pages 91 – 92 and choose one or two values that you want to emphasize in this study.

We've suggested reviewing the Frequently Asked Questions on pages 88 – 90 to gain an understanding of how the group should function and answer any questions that may come up.

Question 3. Also don't forget to give opportunity to get an up-to-date Small Group Roster started during this time.

GROWING. Each Growing section begins with an opening story and a passage of Scripture. Have someone read the opening story and someone else read the Bible passage aloud. It's a good idea to ask someone ahead of time, because not everyone is comfortable reading aloud in public. When the passage has been read, ask the questions that follow.

It is not necessary that everyone answer every question in the Bible study. In fact, a group can become boring if you simply go around the circle and give answers. Your goal is to create a discussion — which means that perhaps only a few people respond to each question and an engaging dialogue gets going. It's even fine to skip some questions in order to spend more time on questions you believe are most important.

Remember to use the Study Notes as you prepare for this session to add depth and understanding to your study.

Questions 4 – 9. Select among these questions to the degree you have time. Groups doing deeper Bible study will want to spend more time with these questions. Others may want to choose one or two questions to discuss.

Following are some notes to help you prepare your answers to these questions. Mary was a virgin, betrothed to marry Joseph, when the Holy Spirit came upon her and Jesus was conceived. Mary did not argue with the angel or express any disbelief; she simply asked him how the birth could take place since she was a virgin. The angel responded with the news that Mary's own elderly cousin Elizabeth was pregnant, too, proving that nothing is too difficult for God. Joseph, who had not seen the angel, tried to leave Mary quietly because he didn't believe — until God came and spoke to him in a dream.

DEVELOPING. Question 10. Here is your opportunity to encourage your group to embrace Scripture reading and time with God by using the Reflections throughout the week. Remind them of how regular time with God and his Word will reap the reward of spiritual growth for those willing to give themselves to it. Maybe you or someone else in the group can share a personal story of the impact this important habit has made on you.

Question 11. For those who haven't done a LIFE TOGETHER study before, spiritual partners will be a new idea. This addresses the practice of having an accountability partner, someone who will commit to pray and hold you accountable for spiritual goals and progress. This may be the single most important habit your group members can take away from this study. Encourage everyone to partner with one other person, two at the most. In this session we encourage you to become familiar with and begin to use the Personal Health Plan to challenge and track your spiritual goals and progress as well as your partner's. There is one Personal Health Plan in the appendix of this book, so be sure to have a few extra copies on hand at your first meeting for groups of three spiritual partners.

SHARING. Question 12. The Circles of Life represent one of the values of the Small Group Agreement: "Welcome for Newcomers." Some groups fear that newcomers will interrupt the intimacy that members have built over time. However, groups generally gain strength with the infusion of new blood. It's like a river of living water flowing into a stagnant pond.

Some groups remain permanently open, while others open periodically, such as at the beginning and end of a study. Love grows by giving itself away. If your circle becomes too large for easy, face-to-face conversations, you can simply form a second discussion circle in another room in your home.

As leader, you should do this exercise yourself in advance and be ready to share the names of the people you're going to invite or connect with. Your modeling is the number-one example that people will follow. Give everyone a few moments to write down names before each person shares. You might pray for a few of these names on the spot and/or later in the session. Encourage people not to be afraid to ask someone. Almost no one is annoyed to be invited to something! Most people are honored to be asked, even if they can't make it. You may want to hand out invitations and fill them out in the group.

SURRENDERING. Throughout this study, we will be discussing various aspects of prayer and encouraging the group to practice a different aspect each week. These aspects of prayer include where and when we pray, praising God through prayer, petitionary prayer, intercessory prayer, how God answers prayer, and unanswered prayer.

Question 14. One of the most important aspects of every small group meeting is the prayer support we offer to one another. The Surrendering section gives you the opportunity to share needs and know that the group will be faithful to pray. As leader, you want to be sure to allow adequate time for this important part of small group life.

Never pressure a person to pray aloud. That's a sure way to scare someone away from your group. Instead of praying in a circle (which makes it obvious when someone stays silent), allow open time when anyone can pray who wishes to do so. Have someone write down everyone's prayer requests on the Prayer and Praise Report. If your time is short, consider having people share requests and pray just with their spiritual partners or in smaller circles of two to four.

Question 15. Every believer should have a plan for spending time alone with God. At the end of each session we have provided Reflections for your group members to use in daily time with him. There are five daily Scripture readings with room to record your thoughts and on day six there is a place to record your summary of the five reflections. These will reinforce the principles we are learning and develop the habit of time alone with God throughout the week.

SESSION 2: YOU CAN HAVE MY SON — ABRAHAM

As you begin, welcome any new people and praise those who brought them. Renew the vision to welcome people for one more week and model this if you can. Then have everyone sit back, relax, close their eyes, and listen to one of the songs on a LIFE TOGETHER Worship CD, or any worship CD. You may want to sing the second time through as a group, or simply take a few moments of silence to focus on God and transition from the distractions of your day.

CONNECTING. Question 1. If newcomers have joined you, take a few minutes to let all members introduce themselves. You could even let each member tell one thing he or she has liked about the group so far, and let the newcomers tell who invited them. The first visit to a new group is scary, so be sure to minimize the inside jokes. Introduce newcomers to some highly relational people when they arrive, and partner them with great spiritual partners to welcome them at their first meeting.

You will get to know each other more quickly if you spend time with an icebreaker question at each session. Use the questions here as a way for bonding within your group.

Question 2. Checking in with your spiritual partners will be an option in all sessions from now on. You'll need to watch the clock and keep these conversations to ten minutes. If partners want more time together (as is ideal), they can connect before, after, or outside meetings. Give them a two-minute notice and hold to it if you ever want to get them back in the circle! If some group members are absent or newcomers have joined you, you may need to connect people with new or temporary partners. In a week or two, you might want to ask the group how their partnerships are going. This will encourage those who are struggling to connect or accomplish their goals.

GROWING. We highly recommend that, as leader, you read the Study Notes ahead of time and draw the group's attention to anything there that will help them better understand the Bible passage and how it applies to their lives.

Question 4. The writer of Hebrews gives us the reason Abraham could go through with this: "Abraham reasoned that God could raise the dead" (Hebrews 11:19). It wasn't that Abraham believed God would provide a substitute sacrifice.

He actually believed that if God told him to sacrifice Isaac, God would have no choice but to resurrect him. God had assured Abraham that the promise would be through Isaac. Abraham was *that* confident about God's word.

Questions 5–6. Select among these questions to the degree you have time. Groups doing deeper Bible study will want to spend more time with these questions. Others may want to choose one question to discuss.

Question 7. Righteous action is evidence of genuine faith. Abraham believed what God said and acted accordingly. No emotion, desire, or worldly pressure could dissuade him.

DEVELOPING. Question 8. Most small groups are not led by just one person. Maybe you've been carrying the whole load so far. Maybe you've opened your home, bought the materials, prepared the refreshments, led the study, and done all the cleanup. That's a huge burden on a leader. And ironically, it also keeps everyone else from growing in their gifts. In order for your group to be the body of Christ, your responsibility as leader is to get them in the game. It doesn't occur to members to volunteer to do things when everything's going fine. They may be thinking they can't possibly do as well as you. It's your job to encourage or even champion every member of your group.

Question 9. Here we talk about rotating host homes. This practice of rotating homes and leaders will help you to spot potential leaders and those who can fill in for you when you are unavailable for some reason. This is an important practice if you are going to help your group develop their gifts and leadership skills.

SHARING. Question 10. Make this a social event a priority. If group members are reluctant at first to invite outsiders, be prepared to get the ball rolling with your own invitations. Ask for volunteers to head up the event planning. If no one volunteers to plan the party, don't be discouraged. Who do you think are the one or two party people in your group? They are likely to respond well if you ask them right after your meeting to take on this project and if you ask two people to team up. Another surefire approach is to ask the group who would be two people perfect for this task.

SURRENDERING. Question 11. We ask that you break the group into smaller circles for the prayer time this week and that you ask your group to focus their prayers on praises to the Lord for the blessings in their lives. Let the group share their blessings within their respective circles and encourage them to use the Prayer and Praise Report to record the praises. Having the prayer requests written down will prompt you to pray for each other. It will also serve as a reminder to you of God's faithfulness as your group sees the prayers answered. After requests have been recorded, spend some time praying in the circles for the requests.

Question 12. We've provided opportunity for a personal time with God throughout the week using the Reflections at the end of each session. Don't press seekers to do this, but every believer should have a plan for personal time with God.

SESSION 3: HOPE FOR THE HOPELESS — RAHAB

If your group is rotating leaders and you're leading for the first time, thank you for your faith. This is the kind of faith step that makes God smile.

In order to maximize your time together and honor the diversity of personality types in your group, do your best to begin and end your group on time. You may even want to adjust your starting or stopping time. Don't hesitate to open in prayer even before everyone is seated. This isn't disrespectful of those who are still gathering — it respects those who are ready to begin, and the others won't be offended. An opening prayer can be as simple as, "Welcome, Lord! Help us! Now let's start."

If you've had trouble getting through all the Bible study questions each week, consider breaking into smaller circles of four or five people for the Bible study (Growing) portion of your meeting. Everyone will get more "airtime," and the people who tend to dominate the discussion will be balanced out. A circle of four doesn't need an experienced leader, and it's a great way to identify and train a coleader.

CONNECTING. Question 1. If new members have joined you, your top priority is to make them feel welcome.

Question 2. Have your members check in with their spiritual partner, and assess how they are doing with their Health Plans and the goals they have set for themselves.

GROWING. Questions 3 – 6, 8. Select among these questions to the degree you have time.

Question 7. For this, Rahab was counted among the men and women of faith in Hebrews 11, and James wrote of her: "Was not even Rahab the prostitute considered righteous for what she did when she gave lodging to the spies and sent them off in a different direction?" (James 2:25). And God honored her through the psalmist: "I will record Rahab and Babylon among those who acknowledge me" (Psalm 87:4). All of this because she trusted in the God of Israel — a God she had only heard about until the spies came to her house.

Question 9. Rahab gave up the life she had lived and went on to become one in the line of Jesus' earthly father, Joseph: "Boaz, whose mother was

Rahab, Boaz the father of Obed, whose mother was Ruth, Obed the father of Jesse, and Jesse the father of King David" (Matthew 1:5–6).

DEVELOPING. Questions 10–11. On November 2, 1979, *Christianity Today* published an article titled "Prayer: Rebelling Against the Status Quo." This title speaks volumes. According to David Wells, in his adaptation of this article in *Perspectives on the World Christian Movement: A Reader* (William Carey Library, 1999), it is "the refusal of every agenda, every scheme, every interpretation that is at odds with the norm as originally established by God." This is what petitionary prayer is all about—refusing to accept things that are against God's will, and instead asking for things for ourselves or others based on God's will for our lives. Knowing how to pray within God's will is challenging. That's why we recommend that you practice praying through Scripture to help you understand what God's will is.

Question 12. Urge group members to encourage each other in their commitment to the group. Each week, ask someone to contact anyone missing from the group meeting. People will really feel loved when your group notices absences and reaches out to those who miss a meeting.

SHARING. Question 13. Take time here to talk about a need that you can meet together as a group. Make this your group's ministry project. Once you identify your ministry project, divide up the responsibilities and determine your plan of action. How will you meet the need? Who will oversee the the project? What responsibilities are left that other group members can do?

Question 14. Return to the Circles of Life to see if the people needing invitations to join the group have been contacted yet. If not, encourage members to make the call within the next twenty-four hours.

SURRENDERING. Question 15–16. Never pressure a person to pray aloud. That's a sure way to scare someone away from your group. Instead of praying in a circle (which makes it obvious when someone stays silent), allow open time when anyone can pray who wishes to do so. Have someone write down everyone's prayer requests on the Prayer and Praise Report. If your time is short, consider having people share requests and pray just with their spiritual partners or in smaller circles of two to four.

There are bound to be people in your group who long for healing, whether physical or emotional, and this will come out during prayer request time. Some churches emphasize prayer for healing—if yours does, follow your church's practice in the way you approach this. Other churches prefer to avoid a charismatic flavor in their small groups—if yours has that concern, pray for one another in whatever way seems comfortable. If you're concerned that some members might confuse or try to "fix" others through prayer, pray as a whole group and monitor how people pray. But don't be overly concerned: the very worst that will happen is that someone will pray in a way that distresses someone else, and if that happens you can simply talk to each person privately before your next meeting. As leader, you set the example of how people will pray for each other in your group, and most members will follow your lead.

SESSION 4: SERVANTHOOD — JAMES AND JOHN

The Bible is clear that every Christian is meant to be a servant of Christ. We strongly recommend that you challenge your members to take whatever step to which they sense God is calling them. You will need to model here. Don't miss the need people have to grow through sharing responsibilities to serve in the group.

CONNECTING. Question 1. If new members have joined you, your top priority is to make them feel welcome. Then be prepared to answer this question first to get the discussion started.

Question 2. In week six, when we will focus on Surrendering, we provide three different experiential exercises the group can choose from to demonstrate their personal surrender. We suggest everyone look at them together and decide which works best for your group. Then assign different members to bring the necessary items. You might want to call people the night before to remind them of the special night. Encourage them to pray for the group and for God to show up in an amazing way. Read the instructions for Communion, Footwashing, and Surrender at the Cross ahead of time so you're prepared for this discussion. Sharing any of these activities in a small group isn't difficult — why not give it a try?

Question 3. As you encourage your group members to check in with their spiritual partners this week, you might want to ask the group to share how their partnerships are going. This will encourage those who are struggling to connect or accomplish their goals.

GROWING. Questions 4–8. Select among these questions to the degree you have time. Groups doing deeper Bible study will want to spend more time with these questions. Others may want to choose one or two questions to discuss.

DEVELOPING. Question 10. In this session we want you to be thinking about this group continuing to meet for another study. Discuss whether your group will continue to meet and what you might study next.

SHARING. Question 11. Scripture commands us frequently to pray not only for each other within God's family but for those who have yet to become members of his family. What better way to show true servantlike care and compassion! Encourage everyone to continue to reach out to the unbelievers around them.

SURRENDERING. Question 13. Remind the group about the importance of spending time alone with God throughout the week. Mention that the Reflections section can be an opportunity for developing this important habit while using this study.

GROWING. Question 3. God is the true king, high and exalted. He is infinitely holy and glorified by all his creation. He is forgiving and wants us to share in his work.

Question 4. Isaiah had pronounced woes (threats of judgment) on the nation (Isaiah 5:8 – 23), but now, by saying "Woe to me!" (cf. 24:16) he acknowledged that he, too, was a sinner subject to judgment. When seen next to the purity of God's holiness, the impurity of human sin is all the more evident. The prophet's unclean lips probably symbolized his attitudes and actions as well as his words, for a person's words reflect his thinking and relate to his actions. Isaiah identified with his people who also were sinful (a people of unclean lips).

Question 6. Live coals were used on the Day of Atonement in the Most Holy Place when sacrifice for atonement for sin was made. Our sin has been atoned for by Christ's work on the cross. Isaiah knew what the coals represented.

DEVELOPING. Question 9. The is a key question, one that demands real soul searching. Be ready to initiate honest sharing and discussion, perhaps with an example from your own life.

SHARING. Question 11. Make sure that the group is moving ahead with possible outreach events/projects. Don't let these opportunities fizzle in the planning stages.

SURRENDERING. Question 12. Share your prayer requests and record them on the Prayer and Praise Report provided on page 70. Have any previous prayer requests been answered? If so, celebrate these answers to prayer.

SESSION 6: HIGHER LOVE—HOSEA

You made it! This is the last session of this study! It's a time to look at where you've been and look forward to what's next for each of you and your group. Your goal for this meeting is to finish strong. It's also a time to think about God's final, ultimate purpose for you: surrendering your whole lives to him in worship, to give him pleasure.

Whether your group is ending or continuing, it's important to celebrate where you have come together. Thank everyone for what they've contributed to the group. You might even give some thought ahead of time to something unique each person has contributed. You can say those things at the beginning of your meeting.

CONNECTING. Question 2. Be sure to have spiritual partners check in with each other at this last meeting. Encourage them to review their Health Plans together to assess where they have grown and where they would still like to grow.

GROWING. Question 3. Whenever we do anything that is unpopular, we risk facing ridicule from family and friends. Hosea would certainly have faced this ridicule as well as the heartache that goes along with the unfaithfulness of a spouse. It's times like these that we discover who our friends and loved ones truly are—who is faithful and who isn't. It's also a time when we discover what is important to others—what drives them. Prepare in advance to offer your own thoughts about this question and be ready to share during the group time. The thing to take away from this question is that, though God asks us to endure hard times, he is with us to sustain our strength and provide endurance to complete the task.

Question 4. Unfaithfulness leads to misdirected gratitude, self-centered motives, misguided actions (we leave God or spouse because the grass seems greener—things aren't going well so I'll return to God or my spouse), and faulty beliefs. We can avoid all this by remaining faithful to what is true and right.

Question 7. God does not withhold his love from us, regardless of what we do. He wants us to return to him, and when we do he embraces us.

DEVELOPING. Question 8. Spend some time in this last meeting preparing your group to move forward. If your group is staying together, hopefully you've chosen your next study; be sure to take the study guides to the meeting. Suggest that the group take another look at your Small Group Agreement to see if you want to change anything for the next study. Are all the values working for you, or is there some way your group could be improved by changing your expectations or living up to one of these values better than you have been? You can make people feel safe talking about things they want to improve by first asking them what they've liked about the group. Set a positive tone. Then make sure people get to disagree respectfully, that everyone understands that they're speaking in confidence and won't be talked about outside the group, and that the goal of any changes will be the spiritual health of everyone.

SHARING. Question 9. Sometimes we simply don't recognize God's answer to prayer when we see it. Other times the answer is "no" or "not yet." Still other times, it might not be the answer that we want. We need to be praying with the right motives.

SURRENDERING. Question 10. Coordinate a time of Communion, Footwashing, or Surrendering at the Cross for your group to share at this final meeting. Instructions for each can be found on pages 100 – 105 of the appendix.

Communion will probably take ten minutes if you have everything prepared ahead of time. It's a tremendously moving experience in a small group.

If you choose to do a footwashing, make sure everyone understands what footwashing signified in ancient culture. It's important to strip the glamor off servanthood. Serving can be dirty and thankless, like caring for small children with messy diapers. Jesus had no self-focused motives for washing his disciples' feet. He simply did it because he loved them and wanted them to learn to love each other in the same way.

If you really want to bring home this message to your group, wash some people's feet as they arrive or during the meeting. If you're worried about people saying no, wash your spouse's or coleader's feet. This will create a memory that you and your group will never forget. One group did this and still describes the evening as one of the most memorable in their group's ten-year history. Have a chair, warm water, soft music, and a stack of towels ready.

SMALL GROUP ROSTER

Name	Address	Phone	Email Address	Team or Role	Church Ministry
Bill Jones	7 Alvalar street L.F. 92665	766-2255	bjones@aol.com	socials	children's ministry

(Pass your book around your group at your first meeting to get everyone's name and contact information.)

Name	Address	Phone	Email Address	Team or Role	Church Ministry

Experiencing Christ Together:

Living with Purpose in Community

Brett & Dee Eastman; Todd & Denise Wendorff; Karen Lee-Thorp

Experiencing Christ Together: Living with Purpose in Community is a series of six, six-week study guides that offers small groups a chance to explore Jesus' teaching on the five biblical purposes of the church. By closely examining Christ's life and teaching in the Gospels, the series helps group members walk in the steps of Christ's early followers. Jesus lived every moment following God's purposes for his life, and Experiencing Christ Together helps groups learn how they can do this too. The first book lays the foundation: who Christ is and what he has done for us. Each of the other five books in the series looks at how Jesus trained his followers to live one of the five biblical purposes (fellowship, discipleship, service, evangelism, and worship).

	Softcovers	DVD
Beginning in Christ Together	ISBN: 0-310-24986-4	ISBN: 0-310-26187-2
Connecting in Christ Together	ISBN: 0-310-24981-3	ISBN: 0-310-26189-9
Growing in Christ Together	ISBN: 0-310-24985-6	ISBN: 0-310-26192-9
Serving Like Christ Together	ISBN: 0-310-24984-8	ISBN: 0-310-26194-5
Sharing Christ Together	ISBN: 0-310-24983-X	ISBN: 0-310-26196-1
Surrendering to Christ Together	ISBN: 0-310-24982-1	ISBN: 0-310-26198-8

Pick up a copy today at your favorite bookstore!

Doing Life Together series

Brett & Dee Eastman; Todd & Denise Wendorff;
Karen Lee-Thorp

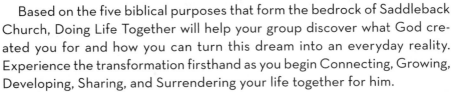

Based on the five biblical purposes that form the bedrock of Saddleback Church, Doing Life Together will help your group discover what God created you for and how you can turn this dream into an everyday reality. Experience the transformation firsthand as you begin Connecting, Growing, Developing, Sharing, and Surrendering your life together for him.

"Doing Life Together is a groundbreaking study . . . [It's] the first small group curriculum built completely on the purpose-driven paradigm . . . The greatest reason I'm excited about [it] is that I've seen the dramatic changes it produces in the lives of those who study it."

—From the foreword by Rick Warren

Small Group Ministry Consultation

Building a healthy, vibrant, and growing small group ministry is challenging. That's why Brett Eastman and a team of certified coaches are offering small group ministry consultation. Join pastors and church leaders from around the country to discover new ways to launch and lead a healthy Purpose-Driven small group ministry in your church. To find out more information please call 1-800-467-1977.

	Softcover	
Beginning Life Together	ISBN: 0-310-24672-5	ISBN: 0-310-25004-8
Connecting with God's Family	ISBN: 0-310-24673-3	ISBN: 0-310-25005-6
Growing to Be Like Christ	ISBN: 0-310-24674-1	ISBN: 0-310-25006-4
Developing Your SHAPE to Serve Others	ISBN: 0-310-24675-X	ISBN: 0-310-25007-2
Sharing Your Life Mission Every Day	ISBN: 0-310-24676-8	ISBN: 0-310-25008-0
Surrendering Your Life for God's Pleasure	ISBN: 0-310-24677-6	ISBN: 0-310-25009-9
Curriculum Kit	ISBN: 0-310-25002-1